JUST WORDS

By: Brian Czarnik

Photos and videos at:

https://www.facebook.com/Justwordsandmusic

TINA!

Thanks for your help + of course your friendship.

-Brian C

25/50

Just words.

First Published 2014. First Edition.

Text Copyright 2014 Brian Czarnik

ISBN-13: 978-1502964953

All lyrics quoted for critical purposes.

Cover Photo: Brian in front of Chicago Picasso 2014. *Taken by: Bridget Czarnik*

Back Cover photo: Brian in the 90's.

So, why write a book?

Why not just put out a damn 8-track, they would sell about the same?

Well, I always thought my life was a little interesting, or at least that's how I perceived it. I figure I might as well get my stories out now, as it seems every year with old age we forget more and more. I haven't played drums or been in a band for a few years now, so it has allowed me just the right amount of space away to reflect back on my musical dream, and the crazy ass times I spent chasing it.

Big spoiler alert, I never made it as a rock star, one of my childhood fantasies, if you also count the fact that I wanted to be a famous explorer who discovered a tribe full of hot naked women. But I hope even with that failure (the music one, not the explorer one, as I am still searching) that there is something in my story that will entertain you—and heck—maybe even inspire someone to go for it.

Whatever their "it" may be.

This is my book about music, dreams, perceptions, and of course, me.

It's just words.

The stuff before the first Section...

The Fox looked at me.

I pulled my frozen hand out of my pocket and took the shot.

I now only had 4 more hours to kill before I could meet Cheap Trick, my favorite American rock band.

Some say, in their wrong opinions, that honor goes to The Beach Boys, Aerosmith, or Metallica, but for me, it's Cheap Trick. My recent habit of taking photos of anything was helping pass the time. I left the fox statue on the bridge over the Fox River in upscale St. Charles, Illinois and continued walking around the town.

I settled in at a Starbucks, because hell, if anyone these days walks far enough you'll eventually walk into a fucking Starbucks. Since I never became a caffeine addict, I seldom remember what drink I get. I ordered a vanilla coffee in medium (not the correct Starbucks language mind you) and sat down to listen to various Cheap Trick tunes on my iPod.

Here I was some 33 years after I first saw them perform in the first concert I ever attended; ChicagoFest 1981. Mayor Jane Byrne's ChicagoFest if you want to be exact.

I can recall riding into the city on that hot August day with my family on the train and having my sister take me to see the band whose record, *Dream Police*, I stole from her just months before the concert. Our parents went to another stage. A stage that had the Oak Ridge Boys "performing," or whatever it is you called what they did.

Chicago was this magical place that had tall buildings that I could see all the way from my backyard ten miles away. And on that day the city was filled with girls and their perfectly feathered hair and tight jeans. The sounds of blues and rock filled Navy Pier along the iconic lakefront.

I was in rock and roll heaven.

Four years later in 1985, I would lip sync Cheap Trick's song "Dream Police" for an 8th grade English class project. I had the Rick Nielsen baseball type cap flipped up, and also leaned into the pretend microphone like Robin Zander. I thought I was badass, but more likely came across like a dumbass.

It was still the easiest "B+" I ever got.

Other kids choose Michael Jackson and we even had a David Bowie, but my selection was the best. I just wish I had learned the words to the middle brake down part, as I had to mouth it worse than Britney Spears.

Back at the coffee shop, I glanced at my watch and walked up to the ticket booth to get my back stage laminate. There is always something about wearing a backstage pass or sticker that makes you feel cooler than everyone else. Feeding the already bloated egos in the rock world is so much fun. I looked at my meet and greet plans and I would have to wait another hour before I could line up to hang out with the boys in the band. Or dudes in their 60's, whichever way you want to look at it.

I returned to my little table and reflected on how cool 1981 was for rock. Not only did I finally get to see my first concert, but a lot of other great music came out that year, all which was blasted from the PA systems in between bands at ChicagoFest. Songs from artist like Billy Squier, The Police, Kansas, and "In the Air Tonight" by Phil freakin' Collins. (See, anyone can sound cool if you add "freakin'" to their name.) The legendary Chicago rock station "The Loop" had a stand there and broadcast the new hits like "Find Your Way Back" by Jefferson Starship to also local rock songs like "Stay in Time/Full Moon" by Off Broadway.

I didn't see much that day. Being a little skinny wimpy shy 10-year-old kid, all I could do was stand on the benches and hope to see one of the band members if everyone in the 30 rows in front of me all leaned to one side. So yeah, I didn't see much.

But I heard it all from "If You Want My Love" to "Reach Out" and of course "Dream Police." I was excited and memorized.

The more I reflected back, the more I felt like I was there again, back in 1981 wearing a dorky jersey concert t-shirt with bad hair and acne. Ah, youth.

Damn, I finally get to line up.

"Everyone with the black pass please wait a while, we have other people first that want to meet the band," barked the security guy.

That gave me the chance to look around the beautiful Arcada Theatre which made me miss the whole performing thing. I would love to play a place like this. They would have to take out all the seats in front of the stage for the rambunctious kids, but after that it would be a nice place to play. Heck, it might even be one of those places that actually pays the bands in real money!

I went over my backstage plan. I will tell the band members that I really like the songs "Up the Creek" and "Invaders of the Heart," two songs that never find themselves on their set list. They will then take me for someone who is very cool and I will not totally geek out and say how much I love the band and all that. I will then make a remark about writing a book which mentions them, and that of course will get them interested in me, heck they will probably ask me to drink with them after the show and talk shop. One of them will offer to write the introduction to my rock and roll book, most likely Rick...what a night this will be!

It will be one of those rock stories that will be forever repeated like the time when Jim Morrison pulled out his pee pee in Florida, or when that unlucky fan got stabbed at a Rolling Stones concert. It will for sure be told on VH1 classic for years to come.

"No autographs and pictures please, we got a guy who will photograph you..."

Ok, whatever, I thought as I tucked my small digital camera back into my jacket pocket. I am too cool for a rock and roll selfie anyway.

The other important people were done meeting the band and now it was my turn. Oh, and the 19 other people with the special black backstage passes as well.

The drunken suburbanite soccer mom in front of me asked the bouncer to hold her beer as she went around the corner and inside the backstage room to meet the band.

Cool, I am next. This will be classic, like Elvis meeting Nixon classic, except totally different.

I saw a photographer snap a photo and out she stumbled. I walked in and noticed Tom and Robin to my left and even before I could say hi to them the photographer said "Ok, turn around."

Fine with me I thought, let's get this picture thing out of the way before I make a funny remark and we all laugh at our rock and roll party that is about to get started. I semi smiled for the photo and turned to nod to the guitarist Rick Nielsen, as I heard the bouncers shout out "Next!"

What? My time is over?

I felt like the kid from the Christmas story when he met Santa, except I didn't even have the time as I was kicked out to rattle off the Christmas list I wanted.

A crew member mentioned to me that Rick just tossed me a pick, so I turned around and bent down to get the pick. I noticed someone else was taking their place with the band for their photo.

Totally anticlimactic, but get used to it, as this is my story of rock and roll after all. And even though I never made it big like a real life rock star, I still had one hell of a journey.

Each section will lead up to the greatest rock story I can possibly tell firsthand.

The story of Oblivion.

The sections may overlap one another on a time frame, but they should all make sense in the end. I have faith in you the reader...you can do it!

"It's all part of my rock 'n' roll fantasy" -Bad Company

The 1970's.

It's funny how as you get older your childhood memories fade to make room for all the adulthood stress and other crap we face like remembering to pay your bills every month. For me the strongest memories of early childhood always centered around music.

Being born in 1971 allowed me to grow up and be shaped somewhat by what was around me and that was what we now call classic rock, otherwise known as the crap that gray haired old people listen to. It's funny: growing up, the classic rock songs were the oldies from the 50's and 60's. Chuck Berry, Roy Orbison, Buddy Holly kind of stuff. As I write this I am hearing the Seattle bands of the early 90's make it onto classic rock playlists. "And here's some Soundgarden from the golden year of 1992."

Shit, that makes me feel old.

It's interesting how many of the groups I grew up listening to are still the same bands who's T-shirts the youth of today are wearing. They just didn't get them from some greasy bootlegger dude outside the concerts like I got them. They buy them new at hip little clothing shops in the mall. Strange world we live in.

I grew up in a blue collar household in the western suburbs just outside of the city of Chicago. Father was a union electrician and my mother, after having me, did various jobs such as lunch room lady and then school bus driver. Yeah, I didn't get my ass kicked too much for my mother being a mean school bus driver. Being the only white boy in many of my early grade school classes made it all too easy for the pissed off kids to find me on the schools playground and throw in a few cheap shots to my stomach. At least little kids back then didn't throw punches to the face. Ah, life was grand back then. One 1970's big ray of hippy sunshine it was. Throw in the fact that I was extremely shy in those early years due to an off-and-on again stutter, and you have the clear picture of a weird little kid. But, being a little off sets the tone of greater things to come. No one should have the picture perfect childhood and be the popular kid. That's just boring. Rock and roll is for the outcasts, the fuck ups, and of course it's for the shy little kid on the school yard getting his metal Million Dollar Man lunch box smashed over his dumb head.

So anyhow, there I was, I had an older half brother and sister from my mom's side who grew up with me in the same house (I had other older half siblings from my dad's side that were already moved out of the house), and music was my best friend. And at most times, my only real friend.

At a young age when given the choice to stay in the car or to go inside and help my mom shop at the local grocery store (Jewel -Osco) my answer was always, "I'll stay here."

In the car I would escape the world around me and listen to the sounds of The Doors, Elton John, The Wings, and Simon and Garfunkel coming out of the station wagon's radio. Being from the Chicago area meant we were always given a healthy dosage of the songs "Lake Shore Drive" and "Bad, Bad Leroy Brown," two tunes that featured the Windy City.

I would sit on the floor of the front seat of the large car and just listen. I would also sit there when the car was moving as this was in a time before seatbelt laws. We weren't pussies back then. Real men ride seat beltless on the floor. Heck, given the construction of those 1970's station wagons, it would take something short of a freight train carrying a nuclear bomb to dent the car anyway.

While growing up a Star Wars kid and a KISS fan (before both these things were retro hipster cool), I would go visit my friend at his house where his older brother had records lying on the floor. We would put on Foreigner, Alice Cooper, and a new band called Van Halen (Van Halen's first record to be exact, which is still their best record). They acted as our sports soundtrack as we played Nerf basketball and hockey in his hallway. There were also the high pitched vocal sounds of Boston, but soon we would harden our elementary school aged taste to Led Zeppelin and AC/DC.

AC freakin' DC. I would spend what little money I got from having a paper route at the flea market on them. That's right I went to flea markets, and many of my early wardrobe was via flea market. Other kids had Puma or Nike shoes; I had "High 5's." Other kids' parents shopped at Toys"R"Us to get the latest Godzilla toy, while I got Dragon Man. You get the picture. I distinctly recall an older woman who always had rock records in milk crates for sale amongst her other junk spread out on an old blanket. It was from her I would buy AC/DC's *Powerage*, *Let There be Rock*, and *Highway to Hell* records. Many a punk rocker seems to be ok with some metal. Motorhead and AC/DC always get a free pass to be cool. And it is for a simple two reasons; they both are simplistic like the Ramones and most punk rock is and should be, and also because they kick ass! If you don't like AC/DC's *Powerage* then you must not like rock and roll.

Speaking of the 70's, I can't even begin to describe how much my mother loved Elvis. We all know that as a kid, you can never like what your parents like. Even as they played Johnny Cash, Willie Nelson and George Jones, which I actually found kind of cool like an old black and white western, I still had to act like I didn't like them. Please keep in mind that I despise modern dumbed down pop friendly country music, and think it makes people stupid. If you don't believe me go to a State Fair sometime!

I had to play it off like it all sucked. But old country music is kind of like beef jerky. Tough to swallow at times, but overall it's kind of good for you. So anyways, there were my parents jamming the 8-track player in our van while we headed off on the big vacation (which was mostly in state or sometimes out of state to Pigeon Forge, Tennessee). Our smaller weekend getaways were either camping just 90 minutes away from home or we would venture across the Illinois/Wisconsin border to the Dells area. Funny how even at a young age I thought places like the Dells and the Smokey Mountains were a little commercial and cheesy for my taste. Now look at those places. They bring tourist trap commercialism crap to a new level. Need a magnet with a cartoon black bear fishing with a pole and a silly hat that says Tennessee on it, well now they have hundreds to choose from along with so many flavors of fudge. They're way too commercial, but some people will like anything.

All of this was just a way to escape. To leave the norm behind. Just like listening to music. Not that I had much to escape from back then. When I was a kid my biggest problem was trying to keep my football and hockey cards dry when our basement flooded. Kids don't have to worry about paying bills and getting divorces. Being a kid is pretty damn cool.

As a kid I had music everywhere I went. If I was outside, I would plug in my tape player with an extension cord from the garage and blast the radio or any mix tapes I made. If I was in bed, I would have the head phones on over my head with the blanket pulled over me, so that my parents wouldn't hear it and tell me to go to sleep. I always avoided sleep like the plague.

One of my first music memories about anything was leaving a toy store (most likely making my parents buy me KISS or Star

Wars junk) and sitting in my aunt's car and seeing my mom in another car, ahead of us, pull off the road. My aunt told me they just announced that Elvis died. It was then I noticed everyone was pulled over.

EVERYONE.

Almost 20 years later, I would be driving to work and hear on the radio that Kurt Cobain had blown his head off. I said an almost silent "that sucks" to myself, but I didn't pull over, and kept driving to my job at UPS. It was big news, and marked the end of the first big wave of 90's Alternative music coming to an end, but no one pulled over. Not a single car.

Say what you want about the fat guy in the glittery jumpsuit, but I doubt when any of us die cars will pull over. Well, unless we die in a car accident in front of them, I guess then they would have to.

We had an upstairs to our suburban house and in a room I shared with my brother during those early grade school years, I would sit and play RUSH *2112* (another gem I bought at a flea market), along with KISS *Alive 2* on 8-track. For those out of the loop on 8-tracks, they had this awesome feature of sometimes fading out of a song midway through it so they could click to another track before fading into the same song. It gave you a moment to reflect on the musical majesty that you were listening to. Music was an experience. I remember lying on the floor next to the turntable and looking at the LP's and reading everything, including the producers, and the record company and copyright year. I was trying to absorb as much as I could from a world that looked so foreign, so alien. Especially that Rush record. Just looking at the guys in their robes seemed liked they stepped off of some space craft not too long ago. A really interesting funky gender bending space craft, but a spacecraft nonetheless. And shit, KISS. Well, as a kid they just blew you away. Even after watching their "what the hell were they thinking" movie *Phantom of the Park*, I still worshiped them. I would pretend I was them on the playground and do this lean back move like Ace Frehley playing his guitar. I thought I was cool, other kids thought I was having a seizure.

I enjoyed the upstairs turntable as the downstairs one was inside this big wooden console. It was hooked up wrong as it would shock the hell out of your fingers when you touched any knobs to turn it on. You really had to weigh out the pros and cons of putting your REO Speedwagon record on.

The 1970's for many was filled with drugs, hippies, bad platform shoes, and disco, but for me I was simply a little brat into rock and roll.

Why do I tell you all this needless info? Well it is to show a simple fact.

I love music in all its craziness. And it also sets the tone for my life.

This is how storytelling works, I think?

"Talk about Pop Musik, Talk about" -M.

The superficial fabulous 1980's.

Who would have thought the early 80's pop music would still be worshipped today as if those fine people in pink alligator shirts and green pegged pants had any answers to life. I still get bitten by the 80's bug and damn if my iPod isn't filled with that musical junk food. Do we glamorize it? Hell yes we do. Like the ex-girlfriend that really wasn't all that great, but when she is gone you look back like she was a sexual goddess. With time, we often make things better than they were originally, to I guess help fulfill the modern depression of growing older minute by minute.

But still, the early 80's were pretty damn interesting. But like anything with a ton of sugar you have to limit yourself, too much will give you a bad tummy ache. Many club DJ's know if you give in and play one early 80's tune you might as well call it a damn 80's night as people go ape shit for that stuff. Even those that weren't their parent's mistakes yet. Or born around then, I guess is the proper way to put it.

Going to grade school during the 1980's, was interesting to say the least just from the clothing options alone. My go to attire were these black tight ass parachute pants I had that I told myself were my version of leather pants. It was in grade school that I was given the chance to choose an instrument. Our 4th grade teacher walked us down to the basement where in a room they had laid out some instruments to choose from. Being the shy little kid, I walked into the room last. I made my way around the tables and glanced over some of the horns as my brother played the trumpet in school band. Nothing caught my attention until the very end where on the table say a snare drum. It might have well been a naked girl sitting there. My eyes grew big as the metal side reflected in the harsh lighting of the room. As I tapped the head the snares rattled and made an interesting sound that I was almost addicted to. As I looked up the music teacher (who was an accomplished violinist) looked down at me with an expression of "oh, hell no." A drummer was born.

I can still vividly remember my brother driving me around in his beat up green Chevy Nova hearing Dexy's Midnight Runners (who many say recorded the 1980's all-time iconic hit with "Come on Eileen") finally reach number one on Casey Kasem's American Top 40 countdown.

Countdowns were fun. Especially the "Solid Gold" countdown that had the hot dancers doing spastic routines to songs, or wasted artist like Ozzy on to lip sync their latest hit. You would cheer for your favorite song to make it up towards number one, like it meant anything to you. Those pop countdowns at the time were infiltrated by mostly wimpy foreign bands like Flock of Seagulls, Men at Work, and even this band that in their video was out in some desert kicking sand talking about jet fighters, The Clash. I obviously in my later years would appreciate much more from The Clash and their importance to music. I wish I was cool enough in the 80's to appreciate punk rock, and I guess I could just bullshit you with stories of how I grew up punk as fuck at Bad Religion shows in California, or moshing it up with Black Flag on the east coast, but I wasn't. I was in my bedroom listening to early 80's sync pop, or after 1983 I was blasting the glam metal bands. In 1983, Def Leppard put out *Pyromania*, (*High N Dry* is actually their best record) thinking at the time that they might be ending their career soon after three great rock records. But, to date, they are still going and have like nine studio records out.

I also took a heavy liking to Motley Crue with their *Shout at the Devil* release. The songs were catchy like the other rock I was listening to, but they also had a heavy almost dirty element to them. And looking at the cover, the guys in the band looked dangerous. I wanted to be them, even with their makeup and strange clothes. Again, I thought this was a band at the middle of their career with this second release. They have to date put out about nine records and are just now calling it quits. What do I know?

I remember bringing *Shout* to this kid who was teaching me how to play a drum set. I asked if he could show me the beat to "Looks That Kill." He strongly disliked metal and thought I should learn some beats from artist like Genesis and Billy Joel. Needless to say my drum lessons with him didn't last long. Nothing against Phil Collins as he actually is a very talented drummer, but I wanted my music a little harder especially if I was going to learn the drums. I wanted to get girls, and it seemed like the guys with the long hair who looked like chicks were the ones getting them.

No offense today to Billy and Phil who have both lost all their hair, and most likely all their hot chicks as well.

So I went home from a few lessons all cocky now that I knew what things on the drum set made which sounds. The basic time in your average rock song was established between the kick drum (thud), the snare drum (the big hit) and the high hat (the chink-chink sound). I was all set. Screw you drum lessons, and screw you Phil Collins wannabe teacher.

I grabbed AC/DC's *Highway To Hell* and self-taught myself rock and roll on the drum set from there on in. I still suggest that record to anyone wanting to learn some basic kick ass drums. In my life I have only taught 1 person to play the drums. They never became a real drummer, but it wasn't my fault. Some say that drummers aren't taught anyway, that we are born this way. A little crazy, a little annoying, but with a great sense of time.

I thought, why hit those things and not get the thrill of playing some hard rock? As around this time that sync pop still dominating the countdowns had lost its edge for me. Metal and bad hair, here I come. Yup, I was a skinny suburban dork with a mullet.

I was also an 80's radio junkie. I didn't mind doing the mindless chores my parents gave me like sweep the leaves off the driveway and then repaint the fence summer after summer as long as the radio was on. And in the 80's if you had a big boom box with dual cassettes you were set for life. I had only a singular cassette recorder, so if I wanted to dub tapes, I had to pick up the one tape player and hold it to the other tape player. So often if you listen closely to my rock radio dubs, you could hear my family yelling at each other in the distant background. I would also have to stay up late at night to dub songs onto tape, as the late night DJ's talked less than the wacky morning or afternoon guys did. That way you could get the guitar intro of the song recorded without having the DJ talk over it until the vocals kicked in. Oh how I hated hearing about traffic or upcoming shows when Yes's "Owner of a Lonely Heart" was kicking in. Staying up late would prepare me anyway for the rock and roll life. And I thought maybe the girls in school would like the sleepy rock star look anyway.

Ah, the damn dumb 80's.

Speaking of cassettes, it was also the time of mix tapes. I remember giving one to a cute girl I worked with at a little grocery store. I thought I had her with many the metal ballads from Bon Jovi and Whitesnake, but I think including Vinnie Vincent's (an ex-KISS guitarist for those of you that are non-metal) "Do You Wanna Make Love" was too much. Not that I would have known what the heck to do with such a hot girl anyway if she took me up on that offer, but it was still a cool song. We never really talked much after my mix tape gift. Simply add her to the long list of females I would freak out in my life time. Well, she is probably some old fat housewife with multiple kids now, and look at me, I'm writing a book.

Along with the candy pop euro bands and glam metal of the time, I was also subjected to the blues. My two older half-brothers were both excellent on the harmonica and also big supporters of the Chicago blues scene. They got me into Rosa's Lounge in Chicago one night to see Billy Branch and the Sons of Blues. Billy is one of the best harmonica players ever. And there is something so basic and honest about the blues. Any band worth their weight will at least acknowledge the influence the blues has had over its favorite bands. Huge powerhouse classic rock bands like The Rolling Stones and Led Zeppelin owe much of their success (and some of their royalties) to the blues.

I would spend hours flipping through my brothers' record collections. Buddy Miles, Big Bill Broonzy, Muddy Waters, and of course Willie Dixon who they had the pleasure of meeting. But as much as I liked looking at the records it was seeing Billy Branch playing live and watching his band (especially the drummer) that stuck with me. The intimacy of the venue and the loyalty of the fans that were there seemed perfect. Something I wouldn't really see again until I started hanging out in the punk clubs a few years later. Well, minus the long sets, as punk rock is good at small intense dosages not two or three long sets of it often including drawn out instrumental jams like the blues bands seem to do. But anyway, back to the 80's pop.

Today's pop music seems nothing more than a reason to give some back up dancers and the makers of auto tune job security. The 1980's had real bands for the most part. Band members that actually played instruments, even if some were those god awful electronic drums and those damn cheesy ass keyboard guitars. In the U.S., we were holding our own with the one and only Devo, a brilliant band who I would dive deeper into their musical catalog later in life. But for now, "Whip It" alone was letting the rest of the world know that we could do this 80's shit as good or as bad as anywhere else in the world.

You can live through so much and only a handful of memories stand out per each decade of life. Songs also have the power to take you right back to a slice of time in your life. One such 80's slice was when I first heard the new single by Foreigner called "Urgent." I remember playing it one summer out of a jukebox at a campground in Kentucky (yup, the family had a big ole' vacation that year) while watching my sister and some local dude play each other in the arcade game Gorf. Space cadet. (Gorf joke...you had to be there.)

Music shaped who I was. I would spend countless hours pretending to be the drummer of Triumph while pounding my drum sticks on pillows before I bought my first drum set. I also spent another set of countless hours prancing around my basement acting like I was the singer in a big rock band, driving the crowd into a fantasy frenzy. That's the power of music for sure. The power to escape and be accepted into this rock and roll mystery planet.

There was something about it all, the cheesy boy meets girl (or somewhat hidden meaning boy meets boy) lyrics. I would attach my own non-existent relationships to these songs and sing them out in my basement bedroom like they were written for me and about me. Now when I mention relationships keep in mind that in my young, semi-innocent grade school eyes, if a girl simply looked at me that meant we were kind of boyfriend and girlfriend. And for some reason if she talked to me or mentioned my name, well then we were so close to doing it (whatever I thought "it" was back then) that I might as well have been walking around with a little rubber on just in case.

I remember going over to my friend Frank's house and following him to his backyard which shared the space with his neighbors. Neighbors that consisted of a daughter lying out in the sun. Too young for side boob, but the fact that she was wearing a bikini pretty much made my day and since she looked up at me as we approached well...like I said, for me good enough. Cheap Trick's "Tonight It's You" became "our" song. Ours in the sense that I liked how this girl looked and could fantasize us living happily ever after from grade six on. And all she did on her behalf was simply looked my way. Naked Eye's "Always Something There to Remind Me" became the more realistic hit for us since this girl was never ever going to talk to me. Yes, I was a creepy little shit, and only had those early 80's tunes to thank for it. Damn you euro keyboards! Damn you!

One time at 1980's band camp...

Halfway through my high school experience I got the chance to twice go up to Madison, Wisconsin and attend a two-week summer band camp at the University. Well, for a high school kid to do anything at a real life college was fun. As a drummer I knew I had to not let anyone down and be the goof off of the band camp sessions. The college kids in charge of our dorms— and in charge of us, acted like drill sergeants in heat. I soon learned that if I bribed my floor manager with leaving him cookies, that I could leave my room messy and also show up a little late to the music classes. I also learned at these classes that the music business had all kinds of jobs attached to it be it producers, studio engineers, lawyers, and of course the studio musicians as well as the lucky guys in the rock bands.

I knew I had finally found my calling. My life up until then was my dreaming of driving trucks on another planet, being a superhero, or finally meeting a hot girl. I had no real direction in life, but band camp gave me a little push towards seeing music as an actual career choice.

I was hooked.

That being said, I didn't disappoint the image of a drummer. My friend and I were the only two kids at camp to be scolded. We had to sit next to one of the university heads at a concert so she could keep us in line. Apparently punching the head of a guy dressed up in a dumb cow suit handing out flyers to some local burger joint wasn't a nice thing to do up there in Wisconsin. We also had the reputation of showing up late for our concerts and not really giving a damn about anything but messing around while most of the other kids were taking their classical music very seriously. From this I gathered that maybe rock and roll musician was the route for me, and not concert band or anything that requires real discipline or talent.

"Here We Are Now, Entertain Us"-Nirvana.

The Alternative 1990's

I will briefly discuss the 1990's as most of my own musical experience takes place in this decade. I don't want to overload on it, but still some things need to be said.

I watch a lot of VH1 Classic these days. Remember it doesn't have to be good to be a classic. I like this current show called That Metal Show. On it many of the metal heads still wrongly blame Nirvana for killing the glam metal of the late 1980's. Shit, that stuff was self-combusting on its own like a hair spray bottle getting struck by a freight train. All along the 80's the underground, indie, punk, and college music scenes were growing and growing. When the music of the late 80's turned to crap, it no longer spoke to us the misguided youth. We wanted to see someone that looked like us up on a stage screaming their brains out. We wanted to feel accepted in sorts by being the outcast generation.

Music comes out, and if it is lucky it catches the ear of the masses. The record companies then think they know what the masses want and sign up or create their versions of the bands playing this "new" sound.

For instance in 1989-1991 when the too late for the party hair bands came out like Pretty Boy Floyd and Steelheart, we (the rock listeners) were sick of light heavy metal (if that makes sense) being forced down our ears and wanted something different. I still remember listening to WVVX (a station that I was on the "street team" for at one time), and hearing how this Seattle band called Soundgarden with its Zeppelin like vocals was stirring up the metal scene. Soon after them, bands like Pearl Jam and Jane's Addiction were being called alternative and the word metal went back to bands like Anthrax, Megadeth and Slayer. Out with the old and in with the new. It's all bullshit trends. Today's unheard of sounds become tomorrow's hipsters' delights. And then it becomes mass media crap selling blue jeans or used in some auto commercials. If you live long enough, you'll see the stupid cycle things follow. Metal, Punk, Dance, Rap, they all have their time in the spotlight. Rock music takes many forms be it grunge, low fi, emo, indie, goth, whatever label they can pin to it and try to sell it to you. For me, it is either good or bad with most music being bad.

Along with the huge success of alternative and punk music came a backlash. Everyone was looking at who would "sell out" next. Green Day took a lot of crap but to me they never really changed their sound as they were always a poppy rock band. It was more of an issue for me of working with a bunch of corporate clueless idiots over your music and your future. I would have wanted as much control as possible with the band. Sticking to your guns meant in many ways limiting yourself in the 90's as music was distributed to stores and this whole download thing wasn't really an option.

On the local front I was lucky to have just barely gotten into the scene before the huge punk explosion. Bands that came in as Nirvana, Green Day, and Rancid were on MTV had to quickly look for some street credibility of sorts as to why they were playing this type of music.

No one wanted to support bands doing it for money, as the scene police were out strong in the 90's. The little rich kids getting dropped off at the suburban shows had to have some issues to deal with ya' know.

The 90's almost had me fooled that things would change. Not only popular music styles, but the way the world worked. I could do my part in refusing to go along with the norm of the music business, and do things my own way. But after a while you realize that for the most part the pursuit of money and the status quo wins and those ideals you have slowly fade away as you find yourself alone fighting whatever issue it is that was once so important to you as a kid.

Just like I did when I was a kid in the 70-80's I would buy records (now indie punk records) and sit and read the record's credits, as well as all the articles I could on bands (now from indie magazines like Flipside and MRR) and daydream on the floor of my room.

The 90's were my 60's. A time of revolution. A time of change. And a time of some damn fine music finally getting the attention it deserved. Until it all turned to crap that is.

"Things seem so different when you got your rose colored glasses on"

- The Bollweevils

I got word from Pete Oblivion that his girlfriend-slash-make out buddy was going to have someone she knew call me about playing the drums for them. Even though Oblivion (who at that time in fall of 1991 had two cassette demos out, and was playing bad metal clubs and still shaping our sound) was taking up all my free time, I was eager to venture out and explore new paths. We all had side projects so to speak, as any crappy musical thing we did with a buddy on a tape was released. Granted most of it was total junk, but fun junk. My big side project hit was the "Chicken Song" with my friend John. We were called Gay Vivian, named sort of after Viv from the British sitcom called the Young Ones. I also had a side stupid band called Popes on Scope. We would also make bad short films on VHS tapes. Yup, we had some free time in college. We often recorded these gems in the wee hours of the morning, and then would force our friends to listen or watch them the following weekend at various dorm room parties. I had trained myself to sleep 4 to 5 hours a night and I would be golden for the next day's routine of college in the morning and afternoon, working UPS at night and then hanging with friends in the late night. I took the "I can sleep when I'm dead" attitude. I wanted to make as much "art" as I could, including songs about sexing up some chicken.

So I get this call from a kid named Ken asking if I would be willing to listen to a tape full of songs and possibly learn the drums on a few. Now before this, my only experience of The Bollweevils was seeing an eye damaging ugly large orange sticker of theirs on the sticky floor of the Metro in Chicago back in July of 1991. I got there just after they played and cleared their equipment from the stage. I picked it up and asked a friend how they were, and he said they were an ok young punk band, nothing special. I dropped the sticker back to its beer soaked home and got into place as we only had one band to go before the mighty Naked Raygun took the stage.

So now this guy from a band that opened up for Chicago punk legends Naked Raygun came over the next day and dropped off a demo tape that featured Ken playing guitars, Bob on bass and singing and their former drummer Joe. I talked with Ken in my basement for a while, and we agreed on what songs to learn and that this Bollweevil band was going to be totally awesome.

As Ken left my house, I instantly put the tape into my beat up tape deck and heard some potentially great music. I didn't love every tune, but I heard something very promising in its simplicity of straight ahead punk rock. I immediately loved Ken's heavy guitar tones. I knew Bob's vocals would be redone with Daryl's as well as I of course would make the drumming even faster. For the next week all I did was listen to that tape if I wasn't at school or at work. These guys were part of a music scene that I was very interested in. They were punks. And I thought if I could be in two bands- well then that would just double my chances of making it as a drummer. It was October 1991, I was 20 years dumb, and I was on my way to becoming a real life punk rocker. Well, a rocker with bad metal hair who was now mixing it with the punk crowd. I hoped no real punker would turn me in to the punk police. Think of how bad that jail cell would smell!

The music was your basic up tempo melodic punk tunes—and I learned all of it—including the ones they didn't play anymore. And just a week later, I found myself unloading my drums (even with those cheesy ass Roto Toms) into Bob's basement in

Forest Park or Franklin Park or actually I think it was Elmwood Park, well, one of those f'in parks, for my big try out.

I met Daryl that day and we all played through the songs. I must have done well enough, because they asked me back to another practice and then another. I soon learned they had a gig just a month after I was given the tape at a college in the Chicago western suburb of Lisle with another young punk band called Not Rebecca. At one of our earliest practices in my basement (at times just myself Ken and Bob due to Daryl's intense school schedule), Ken and Bob pondered the thought of getting Dan from Not Rebecca to sing for the Bollweevils and leaving Daryl with his medical school and its hectic schedule to the side. I was too new to form an opinion on the matter, but felt like I already had a connection with Daryl.

I also wondered if the whole "your lead singer is a black guy" thing was a distraction from the fact that Ken and Bob wanted to be in a punk band that didn't seem like it had a gimmick to it. Most people unfortunately saw a female bass player, an all-girl band, or having someone who doesn't look like most other punkers (white boys) as a gimmick in your band. Life can be so cruel, eh? They also wanted the freedom to tour and become a major player not just in the local area, but in the national punk scene. I could agree to that as we all wanted out of the day to day normal life style and punk rock hopefully would allow us that escape.

Needless to say, nothing to my knowledge ever came from that as Daryl was and still is doing a darn fine job as The Bollweevils front man. I can't even picture the band without his tall figure and head full of dreads with the sweat coming off of him marking his territory on the front of the stage. But it did show me that Ken was the real leader of the band and he was going to have it his way. Punk bands or any bands are seldom a democracy anyway. And that is not always a bad thing.

So we played the Benedictine College gig in Lisle, Illinois. It was fun for me speeding up the tempo and actually seeing a good reaction from the energetic crowd. My mind wasn't solely on the gig as at the time I was "in love" with this Canadian exchange student who went to Pete Oblivion's college. She had to be back in her dorm at a certain time to get a call from her strict father, so I was glad the songs were short because I had to race home and do a 40 min drive in less than 20 minutes. Before I could rush out of there, the guys handed me a Bollweevils T-shirt (that I still have in all its badly stained glory) and told me I was their new drummer. I was excited beyond belief to the possibilities and good times being in this band would bring me.

You could argue that punk rock started with the Ramones and then become the fashion statement and political thorn in the side of the general public with the Sex Pistols circa 1977. So I was going to play what I already considered an older style of music even as punk was only then just over a decade old. Nowadays, I guess it has finally become an older art form, or crappy style of music depending on who you ask.

It didn't take long for that train to leave the station and go full steam. After another mosh pit filled show at Too Far Out Café with a great Chicago band called Trenchmouth. The small back room club filled up quickly with 50 or so people as the loud sound erupted from the band that had Fred Armisen on drums.

Trenchmouth had this hectic, all over the place rhythmic style that took a few listens to get used to. Many punk bands we played with had a repetitive style that by the time the second verse and chorus were coming around, you already had the song in your mind like it or not. But Trenchmouth offered something different than most. At that gig I remember the drummer talking a lot on stage and thinking, "Shit, does this guy think he is a comedian or something?" Well, why yes he was and still is. Portlandia is a damn silly funny show, and Fred's a funny guy on SNL as well as an amazing drummer.

Things got a rolling very fast with The Bollweevils. Not every early show was a hit, but we all worked our asses off in practicing and promoting the band. The Chicago punk scene just had its late 80's wave of bands like Naked Raygun and Screeching Weasel (both of whom had uncertain futures in 1991), but you didn't really see those guys hanging out any longer at these all age shows. We were determined to be a band that was not only playing for the crowd, but also one in the front row for other bands coming up. Sometimes at shows that was the only audience you had—band members.

My bar was set pretty low anyway, so if 10 people came to a show, I was a happy camper. There were only a few places willing to have punk shows and most of them wanted to be familiar with your band or able to hear something first. Since we didn't have any music out yet, it seemed best to invite people over to our practice and treat them like a show. My basement could hold 20 or so people and that was all that would most likely show up to a club to see an unheard of band anyhow. Some friends of ours were starting a band called 88 Fingers Louie, so I also asked them when they had enough songs for a short set to play my basement. I only had a few basement shows with both Bollweevils and Oblivion. When we started to build some interest after playing some clubs, I started to lose track of how many people were in my house (well, my mom's house, filled with all her collectable dolls). It took me hours to look over the house and put back the dolls that kids had put in various sexual positions. And the neighbors were wondering what all the cars parked on my street were for.

One weekend afternoon, my day started with finding this street-looking punk sitting in my drive way. How he got there I will never know as there was no public transportation around in Hillside. I asked if I could help him and he said he was hoping I was having a show tonight as he heard this basement place was cool. I told him I didn't have anything scheduled and he just started slowly walking away down my suburban block.

Even though some of the shows were poorly attended, we could see the fan base building up after every gig, as well as our playing seemed to get tighter and tighter. For me it was also a chance to branch out. With hanging out with my Oblivion crowd I was being subjected to a lot of different kinds of alternative music and metal, but these Bollweevil lads seemed well schooled in indie and punk music. From just looking at the shirts that Bob wore, I got turned on to (not turned onto little Bobby, but you know what I mean) several bands like Jesus Lizard, Superchunk and Jawbox.

Speaking about shirts, we put in hard work silk screening our own shirts and practicing our punk tunes over and over. Even from an early point we had the balls to play several Raygun and Effigies covers, along with "Silly Girl" from the Descendants, and "Fast Cars" from the Buzzcocks. Lucky for us I think the people at the shows knew we were just playing songs we liked and in no way were trying to compare ourselves to any of these punk legends. You could piss people off very easily in the touchy punk community, and to come out and think you are equal to one of the past greats is not a good way to start off your band's image. So we made it very clear, even down the road as we released the cover songs on various CD's and 7 inches that it all was done out of respect for some great past songs, and we weren't trying to pass it off as look at us we can be just as good as Raygun. It was a different era for sure. Speaking of Raygun, Pierre Kezdy, their bass player, was nice enough to have us over and talk to us about music and the local business of it all. Pierre was one of the nice soft spoken people in a scene of many who acted very differently. It was also nice to see someone for who they were off the stage, as for me this music thing was going to be my life, and I wanted to know everything about it. So to know how a person was off-stage was for me just as important as the persona on-stage. I was also glad to be accepted by the local punks, as early on I still felt like some spy as I was coming from a different local rock scene all together.

Things from then on seemed to keep going our way very fast, and before I knew it, people would come to the shows and sing along and request our early songs like "Finale" and Talk" that we were going to play anyway. We also had this Sludgeworth groovy (remember their funk songs?) little number called "Stained Glass" that made its way onto the Underdog Actung Chicago! Zwei. Screeching Weasel was on the first comp with the Dry Heathens, so yup, it was very cool to be on the new second edition. The song "Stained Glass" would later become a joke a year or two later as the longtime fans would request it to no avail. We didn't see the need to move forward using the funky style anymore and preferred the fast-driving or heavy mid tempo songs. Plus, we weren't big on the funky stuff to begin with, ours or anyone else's for that matter.

In February of 1992 we found ourselves in the studio to record a few 7 inches. To me this was a dream come true as my only other recording experiences up until this point were the two demo tapes I did with Oblivion. I thought Ken told me that they work with this guy Chuck U-'Cheetoh" up in some Attic. How punk rock, an attic!

All these punk guys took on silly names or the name of their bands like Joey Ramone, Joe Queer, or Ben Weasel, so I though wow this Chuck guy must really like Cheetos! What a lover of tasty snacks he must be. It wasn't until I met him that I realized Ken said Chuck Uchida.

Meeting Chuck was one of the best things that ever came out of me playing in The Bollweevils. As I write this, he still is one of my good friends, and I have spent countless hours talking music at the late great Chicago bar Club Foot, among other places.

The first 7 inch contained the songs "Lost and Found" and "About You" (we would mess with this song's tempos again a few years later, but this first version is probably better). The feeling of finally getting your music out on vinyl was awesome. I felt like anyone can make a tape, but vinyl, it's so permanent, after all vinyl was on the same format of all my favorite music that I would play in my room as a kid growing up. It was for sure a milestone in my little career to finally be on vinyl. The same format I sat with in my bedroom and daydreamed about me being a musician just years before. And I didn't even have to wear funny robes like the guys in Rush did.

I was on my way to becoming a real live rock musician. Even later when we would record a full length vinyl record, and have CD's and tape versions as well, I would always personally listen to the vinyl version. Come to think of it, I was a cool little hipster before hipsters fell in love with vinyl records. I was way before my time. So this red vinyl 7-inch came out on our own label, something Bob and Ken called Go Deaf Records.

The cover was done by Attica resident Markus (who would later design the first two Oblivion records) featured some random kid's head on it. When we had shirts made with the head, everyone thought it was Bob. I got a stupid kick out of agreeing with people that it was indeed Bob and he was just shy about letting people know it was his face on our record and shirts. The 45 record also came with a booklet of assorted art, including my friend John (and also my bandmate in Gay Vivian) who drew an instructional cartoon of "How to Vomit."

Our friends were such an important part of the band. They came to the shows and always got the crowd going. Friends like these guys Nick, Jimmy, C.J., Mike, and then Joe and Dennis from 88 Fingers Louie. They all cheered us on when we played, but often busted our balls after the show when we all went out to eat. I will never forget those early days and the guys who made it such a fun time. I never was sure what they made of me. I stood out a little wearing my goofy shorts and metal shirts when blue jeans and black shirts with your favorite band on them were the suggested scene outfit. These guys were a blast to be around.

Many times in my career, I would see where it only took one or two kids to start jumping around to get the entire crowd jumping or the pit slamming around. People in crowds are such followers. Even the punk crowd which prides itself on being all individuals. Yeah right. We all want some kind of clique to take us in. And at shows where no one was willing to be the first, our gang of friends always jumped right in.

Soon after that first 7-inch came out, our second one (on Chicago punk label Underdog Records) followed in 1992. It was called *Disassembler EP*. Ken ripped the title idea and the cover art from some other local band. I felt too new in the band to voice an opinion on the matter. I thought it was funny anyway, and had to explain it to the original band when their singer emailed me (this was the early days of free AOL email mind you) a few times about it. Pissing people off is very punk. Don't forget that. When a big magazine at the time, Alternative Press, did a story on the two bands and our similar 7 inches they liked the other one better anyway.

The four songs ranged from our soon-to-be-token fast sound to some mid temp songs like "American Savior" and "No Time." Even though I always felt like we were at our best with the faster poppy stuff, these songs for me to this day are a nice change of pace if you will to the normal Bollweevil sound. One of the best things about that second 7-inch was the bad photo on the back cover taken at the end of a Taco Bell drive in where I went to a million times.

Speaking about friends, nice segue eh? Ken and myself (who haven't spoken face to face since 1997) actually took a road trip together in summer 1992 to check out the California music scene. We also wanted to get a feel for the road, as we knew the Weevils (I always hated that "Boll" part) would tour soon enough. It seemed many a bands were "making it"—getting their records out on California labels and the whole punk thing was growing thanks to Cali bands like Green Day and Jawbreaker, so we felt obligated to go check out what all this California punk talk was all about. What we didn't do (and this I realized somewhere in Kansas) is have a plan of attack.

We first stopped the car in Berkeley and hung out at the campus. We watched as this street performer ranted about social and political issues and all that. He passed out cards and we learned his name was Stoney. He became the reason for one of the best Bollweevils songs ever in "999-Stoney." That song would come out the following year in 1993, and appear on our third 7-inch record called *Ripple EP* with a great cartoon drawing of us as mid-life crisis drunks on the cover. As I look at the artwork now I am glad I don't resemble that drawing too much, as I still have most of my hair. That 7 inch would be our last for Underdog Records as well. So after having no one talk to us on that campus we felt like losers and went to spend a night in a dirty, drug-infested hotel in the Oakland area. I rushed to get into the shower to wash off miles and miles of dirt. I stupidly also scratched away some scabbing off a recent tattoo on my shoulder I had gotten days before we left.

We got up the next day hoping to see a 924 Gilman show, which at the time was ground zero for west coast punk rock (with CBGB's being the East Coast Mecca.) It was just our luck that a club that was hosting a million shows at the time would have no show that night, so we made our way across the bridge to San Francisco for a few hours to hit some record stores. Even though we couldn't find our own records in there we knew someday we would have a release that would find its way into the punk stores one way or another. Since we had no money we didn't spend long shopping and soon decided we would make our mark in Los Angeles. Again with no plan, and with no place to stay.

We made it down to LA which still had a strange vibe to it as the Rodney King riots had taken place just months before. So there we were two white stinky kids from the Midwest standing in line for some fast food in the East L.A. area. I remember looking up at the helicopters and remarking how I saw helicopters like that in the movie *Boyz n the Hood*...duh, as some older homeless guy told us we should really get the hell out of the area we were in. Which we did, after we got our food. Nothing stands in the way of food on a road trip. Now in the safety of Ken's little blue car we ate our burritos and argued about how long to make our working vacation (which was going oh so well).

We later spent the night on Hollywood Boulevard. It was not the glamorous Hollywood that I hoped it to be.

We both had little missions we had to do. Mine was trying to forget about the foreign exchange student who had just broken my wimpy little heart over the summer, and Ken's was to pee on Capitol Records in an effort to stick it to the man. I was doing a crappy job on my mission but we did somewhat succeed on Ken's as we found that iconic building and he had to settle for pissing on the security gates around it. To my knowledge they weren't electric fences, as Ken made it back to the car after the deed was done. We then parked and walked down to spend the night on Hollywood Blvd in hopes of being discovered or something, cause that's how Hollywood works right?

As I sat on the cement sidewalk that was filled with stars and looked up at some more real ones, I pondered what every 21 year idiot thinks about and that is, *what's it all about*?

I learned two things about myself and Hollywood that night. One, that around 4am they start cleaning those damn stars, so if you are sleeping on the street or rather sidewalk, you can get a free bath. And lesson #2 well nothing to learn really but the experience of having some street kid pulled a gun or a lighter in shape of a gun and point it at my head. I made no moves, either way I could have cared less on this highly unproductive trip. After we snuck into the football field locker room showers in U.C.L.A. for a quick washing, we raced all the way across the western U.S. in his compact car and back to Chicago the next day and called it all a big waste of time. But we still somehow knew California and all it offered would play a major part in the band.

We played a few more shows the next few months including opening for the very popular Chicago band Screeching Weasel at McGregors in February of 1993. The lackluster response to us at that gig showed us we still had some climbing to do to win over a big crowd. We only saw these big crowds when the bigger names in punk came around. As for your average all no name local band shows, we would be happy to play in front of 25 people. But we kept at it, like slowly pulling teeth to get more people out to hear us. We kept practicing in my basement whenever we found time in between our jobs, college, and hanging out with all our friends at record shops or shows.

Our road trip fever for sure took its course and we all soon asked off from our jobs for two weeks (pretty much the maximum amount I could take off from UPS. at that time, so it was a good thing Oblivion wasn't touring yet) and planned our first real tour during July of 1993.

The month before we planned our first long road trip to see if we could all get along in a van. This newer music festival North by Northwest was trying to continue for its second year and wanted to become something like the popular South by Southwest held in Austin, Texas. But the only problem was the NxNW festival was being held in the woods of Lolo Montana. That's right, where the hell is Lolo, Montana? Now a days one would google map it and kindly tell the show organizer a polite "no thanks," but this was 1993 and a young band that was hungry for any type of show. Let alone one that a promoter was promising thousands of music loving fans and also there could be major label record scouts there as well. And the best part is that we would get a check for $100! (That huge hundred dollar check actually bounced later but let's continue.)

We rented a small van, loaded our crap into it, and took off for our 24-hour drive to Lolo. We got there on day two of this three day festival, looked around at a bunch of camping hippies and were told we go on just before 6pm. I should point out here that I disliked hippies. It's a punk thing to do. I figured they had their time to change the world and due to them being all peaceful on pot, they fell short. I thought with this new early 90's punk and alternative revolution that we had a better chance to really over throw the system than they did. I looked over the field of hippies before me with much distain. We checked out this pop punk band 49 Reasons from South Carolina and then watched as slowly people awoke from their tents. We all brushed our teeth and met with the organizers and a pretty girl who said she worked for some big record label. There weren't thousands of bodies there (unless you counted all the bears in the woods watching) but a few hundred. And the music was mostly jangly wimpy rock. We took the stage, announced that we were The Bollweevils from Chicago, and ripped into our fast pace set. During the first song, some long haired dude comes running to the front of the stage and holds up his fist and then rams his head onto the elevated stage's wooden floor and then passed out. That was Lolo.

A month later for our big 15-day tour to the west coast and back, we had our first three 7-inch records along to sell (that's 21 inches of punk rock mind you.) We felt like it was time to branch out from being just a local band to hitting the road and exploring the west. Going with us on our mission was Pete Mitler (aka Pete Heathen, who we knew from his band the Dry

Heathens who had appeared on the Actung Chicago! Record as well). Pete had a van and was willing to travel. So yeah, he was in. Pete nowadays is the fill-in bass player for Naked Raygun, but on that tour he was our driver. Our red headed chauffer to hell, if you will. Also along for the ride was our friend Joe from 88 Fingers Louie. Joe hopefully now travels in better style with his current and more popular band, Rise Against. But back then, he fit perfectly in our crowded van of smelly misfits.

We even found a touring partner in the Smoking Popes. That band was yet another connection we made through the Underdog Records Actung comp, as they played with us at the release show at the local suburban club McGregors.

McGregors would host all age punk shows and booked young punk bands like Jawbox, Green Day and Jawbreaker back in the early 90's. I had seen the Popes a few times and loved their pop sense mixed with sarcastic punk attitude. Josh had even written a song "Ruebella" in which Daryl would sing back up on this tour. Before the tour I got to hear Josh sing KISS's "Love Gun" at Daryl's apartment with an acoustic guitar. I was looking forward to hanging with the Popes. Anyone who can pull out a KISS song is a friend of mine. And everyone needs some form of religion I guess. As a retired Catholic, I would count touring with a band that had the word Popes in it as if I was going to church, it does a soul good.

What a cast of characters we had for my first band tour. A tour was anytime you had more than like a week of shows on the road. Anything shorter than that was just a simple road trip, so this was finally a tour! I didn't know what to expect. Would it be like what I anticipated it to be from all my early youth rock and roll tour diary reading from magazines like Rolling Stone, Circus, and Hit Parade? Would it be like Led Zeppelin with crazy hotel parties with squid fishing off the balcony and lots of rock chicks at every show? Or would it be like some of those tour diaries I was reading in the punk rock magazine MaximumRocknRoll, in which a van breaks down and the band starves and has to eat an unlucky band member to stay alive. Or worse than that, no one comes to the shows! Only time would tell. And the time felt just right for a local band that only had a few 7 inches and pressed some t-shirts to bring our show to the masses on the west side of the U.S.A.

Our first stop was in nearby Beloit, Wisconsin. A nice crowd showed and supported both bands. We weren't that far from home, but back then the Chicago area had a strange way of splitting up its scenes. For instance you would have your Chicago kids, your Elgin kids, the Rockford scene, and your near west suburban kids. But for them to cross the state line and attend a Wisconsin show might be asking too much.

The following day we played in St. Paul, Minnesota in a basement with the local band there called the Quincy Punxs. It was a blast, and I soon learned that having 20-30 kids packed in a basement is way better than playing in some big club that felt empty with 50 or so kids in it. Also at these basement shows, you could often sleep at the house you played at. And the vast majority of any money collected was given to your band, which meant the gas tank on Pete's van or off to some local store to buy cheap pasta and some generic brand pasta sauce. Staying there was my first exposure to a punk house. Or you could call it a beaten down old place that a lot of punk kids crammed into and tried to make rent.

In one of my rare moments using a camera back then, I have this nice photo of the Popes and us all sitting in front of the house we played in Minnesota. We still looked happy as the tour was only beginning. Our drives from that point on were long and hot and the 6 of us packed that van made it hard to sleep as if you closed your eyes you had 5 other guys trying to mess with you. Most of the time was passed trying to listen to these new bands at the time called Rancid and Face to Face on the old tape deck I brought along. The tape deck wasn't really strong enough to overpower the sound of the wind crashing in from all the open windows, but we did what we could.

Daryl and Bob would also sing words to various Smiths songs – I had no idea what they were. I longed for a chance to throw in an Iron Maiden tape, but I was passing my time mostly by sitting up shotgun and talking about girls to Pete as he raced his old van along towards the western coast at illegal speeds.

We then ventured past the Badlands in South Dakota and into Montana. Now some would laugh at the thought of playing anywhere in Montana, but punk rock was funny, as these little towns would have a scene of bored kids that would flock to shows sometimes by the hundreds. I guess in towns that you could either sit in a field and watch some horses take a dump all day, or go see some big city fuck ups play rock, you acted rebellious and went to the rock show. In many a small town in the Bible belt or out in the sticks, a touring musician was seen pretty much as a devil worshipper. And if you had any tattoos or dyed hair, you were a fancy little devil then.

When you're rolling into a town like this in an old van, you might as well be riding up on a horse wearing a dusty black hat. I loved the feeling of being an outlaw, being someone different. Before that Montana show we watched out a window as the old man janitor of the hall took a piss by the dumpsters and wondered when the rock and roll lifestyle would begin? That show would be the first touring gig so far that girls would come talk to us after our performance. It was then I learned the pecking order of the after show events. Girls want to go for the singer, then the guitar player, what's left will talk to the bass player and then the bottom of the barrel zombie types will talk to the drummer (who is most likely still packing up his gear). And in the punk community back then you had even fewer girls. It was more dudes who want to talk about other shows they have been to. But again the pecking order goes the same from interesting guys (like someone who saw Black Flag back in the day) talking to the singer. Then the average concert goer (someone who loves Bad Religion) chatting with the guitar players, and finally the drummer usually gets to hear from some kid that will tell you about the time he once saw the Village People at a State Fair, but that he got sick off of some bad fried pickles half way through the Y.M.C.A. dance. Fascinating.

After that show we were invited to go hang out with some local boys. Since we were new to this touring thing, we thought the more people we could meet, the better. So after we sold some of our merchandise to the kids and packed our gear up we followed this car into a very secluded trailer park area of no man's land Montana. Sounds like the beginning of some bad horror movie. We walked into this kid's house and by the insane amount of beer cans tossed around it seemed as the party had started way before we got there. We walked down to the basement and noticed this huge Swastika flag hanging up. Everyone seemed nice enough at first, but we didn't want to stay and see a few calm skinheads turn into racist crazy skin heads (I say racist as not all skin heads are racist, as the majority of the ones I have met are anti-racist and just normal people like you or me just with very easy to maintain haircuts) so we turned around and walked briskly back to our van. On the way outside the house we saw the Popes going in and told them of the situation. Later that night we met some nice guys who were also at our show and laughed off the stupidity of it all. Who in their right mind would actually want to be proud of such a horrific group like the Nazis, but the punk scene had all kinds in it, even the Montana scene.

Racism is something that we thought we would have to deal with more, but gladly the average punk kid was a little more accepting than most. Being exposed to gay bands, Riot Grrl bands, or bands like us that had someone different than they were. This is not to say that the Montana incident was the only time we came across something odd. For me to comment on this probably isn't the best as Daryl would have been more open to what was going on than his dorky white drummer. I often laughed when kids would come up after having heard us on some CD compilation or something and finally seeing us live and they would say, "I didn't know your singer is a black dude, he doesn't sound black at all." Like if you're an African American musician you have to come out as a Flavor Flav hype man with a "yyaaahh boyyyy, what's up mothfuckas!" Somehow that wouldn't have fit with our band. But I did see a few times in which I thought, "Well that's fucked up."

One time it was while we were all at a truck stop in a small town just out of Knoxville. We always got strange looks when we went out, but this time it seemed the looks turned to stares, some long hard stares from the locals at the bar. Our food came out and then a lot, lot longer Daryl's lunch finally came out. Could it be only coincidence, who knows? We joked about it and told him that every country cook in the surrounding area had probably come over to spit in the food before they brought it out. We also played Springfield, Illinois (why that town is our state capitol, I will never know) and before our concert there was a gathering of a local racist group. One of the main kids came up to us saying he didn't want any trouble, and actually liked our band a lot. He put a strange wig over his bald white head and joined in the pit. Maybe after our show he would see the world in a different way, who knows what makes people realize there are good and bad in everyone, no matter what shade of skin color you're born with.

From there it was up and through Washington State, which was still spinning in all its Grunge glory and for having Nirvana and Sub Pop Records. Of course with anything that was popular, there was a backlash, and those kids that didn't want to be in anything popular were coming out to the punk shows as Green Day's *Dookie* was still six months away. So punk rock, for the most part, was out of the mainstream's eye at this point. From the soaked Northwest we ventured down to California were the van finally called it quits in the hills before L.A. Now we're on tour! The van always has to break down, and for that you bring it into some overpriced auto shop that sees the out of state plates on your vehicles and just knows they have you by the balls. So after overpaying for our little balls to get it out of this crazy auto shop we raced to play at Frank from Vodoo Glow Skull's store Cheap Guy Music with Face to Face who was breaking out into the national scene after their debut record.. After that fun filled show we raced to Arizona for a gig and then to the surface of the sun or Albuquerque, New Mexico. It was there I soon realized that these punk shows often took place in the worst parts of town.

We were loading up on sports drinks at the local Albuquerque 7-11 and saw some of the tallest prostitutes I have ever seen outside hanging with the local cops. I doubt they would use that as their State motto on their license plates. New Mexico: The Tall Hooker State. We drove over to play a place simply called "Shithouse."

Nothing could have said it better. This was when The Smoking Popes drove up, looked the situation over and told us they were done with the tour and that they might join us for one last show in Arkansas or Missouri or they might not. I wished they would stay, as I liked having them around. I always enjoyed hanging out with others so as to not get burnt out by spending so much time with your own bandmates. And also the Popes entertained me with their simple ways of things. We didn't have time to worry about another band as we were doing our best just keeping ourselves entertained and light hearted given the various situations we were in.

As I was setting up my drums on the make shift Shithouse stage against the front window, I noticed a small hole in the glass. One of the kids there told me that they had a drive by shooting not too long ago.

I played that whole show hunched over a little in the ready to be shot in the head position, if there is such a thing. The next day after a hot five hour drive we wound up in Pueblo, Colorado which would be the highlight of that first tour. We were playing a basement with two bands that were escaping the Seattle scene for a while along with some other touring and local bands. The hosting family made us some of the best Mexican food I ever had, and it was then I realized some of the best part of touring was not only looking out a van window as mile and miles of land passed you by, but meeting people and hearing their stories. We hung out all day swapping tour stories with the bands at this kid's house waiting for the late afternoon to start this little music fest. It seemed that many of the kids were anticipating this "Weevil" band from Chicago to play. Somehow word of mouth had hit this Pueblo town which was impressive back in the time before everyone was on the internet.

We ripped into our set and the basement went crazy. It was a perfect night, which we all needed. We even had some local girls take us back to their place to spend the night. And by spend the night I mean find a few feet of space on the floor and crash. If you got "lucky" it meant that you somehow managed to eat a little pasta and maybe, just maybe brush your teeth and put on some deodorant. No hanky panky here, but that was all right as the homemade refried beans, guacamole and tortillas I had earlier in the day well made up for the lack of sex on this tour. And by lack of, I meant absolutely 110% none.

The next morning we stepped over the other sleeping bodies and got a quick tour of the town and said our goodbyes as we drove to Arkansas and then to Missouri to play our final shows. All in all the first Bollweevils tour was a success in which we realized people from outside the Chicago area could like our band. Speaking of things taking place not in Chicago, Ken had somehow secured us a little record deal with California's Dr. Strange Records, since Underdog Records seemed to have too much on its plate and we wanted to put out another 7- inch fast as Ken and Bob were writing catchy songs faster than we could play them. Well, almost faster. Dr. Strange around this time had lost Face to Face and was looking to not only gain a band, but to branch out with promoting this new Chicago band.

Word of this move didn't take long to go from punk magazine writers to scene critics to other jealous bands. We were getting a little backlash when some people learned we would be putting out records with a California label. One local 'zine said we might as well move to LA as we were sellouts for being on a California label. We could have stayed true in their eyes to the Chicago scene if we waited longer for Underdog Records who was heavily backlogged or we could say fuck it and go with someone who could put it out faster and also be able to distribute it more. It was an easy choice for us. Anyone who knew us, knew we were more than proud to be a Chicago area band (look at the cover of our split 7-inch of *Viva Chicago* for Christ's sake), and we were not willing to become a so-called "California" band. There were plenty of those in the early 90's. And most of them seemed to be on Dr. Strange, Fat, Lookout, or Epitaph Records.

There's something about places like LA and New York. They still have that image of if you are from there, you are the real deal. We wanted to help make Chicago the real deal. Yet did we know that in a few years it would be the cool place and that would play out to be more of a curse than a blessing.

Ken and Bob wanted a new sound for our new label so we left Chuck and recording in the Wicker Park attic and headed to Indiana. They wanted to try out Mass at Sonic Iguana Studios who had just recorded more known bands in the scene like Screeching Weasel and The Queers.

The result was our *Chicago EP* (again making it known that we were not moving to LA), which had the perfect tour song "Dysomnia by Design" as well as two other fast pop punk tunes.

With this slightly more polished sound as well as being seen as a more national band (after all we had played the west coast and were on a California label now which equaled the big time in many a young punk fan's jaded eyes) our local shows grew in attendance with every show we played closing out that year.

The Chicago alternative and rock radio stations were now playing some punk rock on their local showcase shows. The local shows were usually home to local acoustic guitar driven jangly rock, as punk was pretty much ignored. The few good college stations was where any punk band had any hope of getting played, but now things were different and the DJ's didn't want to seem out of touch. Most were though as when some stations formatted over to alternative music, they treated it just like pop music with having a play list of the 20 hits of the day. They would play those songs over and over until you hated them. In those times you might even have heard a song or two from the local bands during regular rotation. This one station, Q101 played the entire local punk Christmas 7 inch that both Bollweevils and Oblivion were on. The Chicago area air waves were taking notice to the growing local scene. We couldn't be ignored for much longer.

The Bollweevils were even interviewed by 1970's TV's former Partridge, and at the time recovering junkie, Danny Bonaduce. He wanted to make fun of little punkers and we kept on the Partridge Family. In the end it served its purpose to help promote a couple of our shows.

The New Year 1994 would start right where the last left off. I was heavily involved in the scene with both bands. The Bollweevils got a nice review of our *Ripple* 7 inch in the Chicago Sun Times, so when the major papers writers start taking notice, you know you are getting there. My own writing for smaller publications was keeping me busy, and through my reviews of the bands Screeching Weasel and The Vindictives, both Ben Weasel and Joey Vindictive were people I came to know. I felt like I was in some elite punk rock inner circle until I went to their places (at the time they both lived in the same building) a few times and realized we all were struggling to keep our music dreams alive, no matter how popular the bands we were in seemed to be at the time.

Ben had a few touring bands call me about shows, and when Jawbreaker (who was one of the best) called me, I jumped at the chance to open. The Bollweevils played with them in March, and it was yet another opportunity for us to build a bigger audience. The town of Homewood, Illinois was putting on some packed shows at a small club called Off The Alley behind a record store. I am sure fire codes were broken that night, but everyone seemed to have a good time, even as they gasped for air in the humid room. You could gauge how full the show was by trying to look through the foggy windows from the side stage room to the main floor. It was in this off stage area when I saw Blake from Jawbreaker tuning up his guitar hours before the show. I always had a habit of getting to shows early, and when it was just he and I in this back room I thought I would tell him how awesome his band is and all that. I remember just nodding and thinking maybe he likes these quiet moments without people around, so I kept my comments to myself. Later on as I would get burnt out at times on the road, it was indeed nice to have a quiet moment with your instrument or sitting alone as it gave you a chance to gather your thoughts as to why you got into this in the first place.

With recording what would be *Stick Your Neck Out* and doing the weekend warrior thing around the tri state area, The Bollweevils decided it was time to take this act to the dirty south in June of 1994. I should mention Scott and Pete Oblivion were being more than nice with planning our shows around the Weevils local shows as well as my leaving for touring. I was doing my best to juggle 2 bands, school, and working nights at UPS and failing at relationships. That short 10 day tour featured us opening for Rancid in Georgia and in

South Carolina. We also brought our friends in 88 Fingers Louie with us to keep us company and help us get the word out that Chicago was home to some decent punk rock bands. This time Joe wouldn't have to ride with us and be smashed into our van, he could be smashed up against, Dom, Dennis, and Dan now, the Triple D's.

Rancid was rising quickly in the punk scene and being on Epitaph Records was many a young punks' dream label. Everyone seemed to love their first record (on Lookout) and of course Tim's former band Operation Ivy, a band my non punk ass never heard of.

We met the Rancid guys at Crazy Johnnies house in Georgia. This promoter Johnny was known for putting on good shows and treating bands nicely. A rarity at the time as most touring punk shows were last minute thrown together messed up evenings or they just didn't go on due to the kids not having a permit, the club not knowing about it, or the cops showing up. Remember punk rock was not in the main stream just yet at this time. Rancid shirts weren't always sold at the mall, ya' know.

One of the perks at the time was that Johnny worked at a local Augusta Hooters. So for lunch before gathering to meet Rancid at Johnnies place we all went to this orange paradise. Picture a bunch of hot southern girls not talking to the stupid looking punk kids who are eating with a guy they know, and you would have just painted yourself the actual picture. No rock and roll sex stories in chicken wing batter here to tell.

When we finished our nutritious meal we all went back to Johnnie's apartment before going to the gig. Even in the punk scene you have people that will act a certain way. The more popular the bands, the more jaded the members can get. As much as we all want to act normal, sometimes when you meet someone in a band you like a lot, you can act really stupid, either helping to feed the already bloated ego a rocker might have or acting like a freak and making the band member want to be anywhere but there talking with you. With that being said, even though Rancid was one of the most up and coming popular bands in the scene at that time they were all very nice. So there we were all crammed into Johnnie's living room. I noticed the trap of everyone laughing at anything one of the Rancid members said, so I walked out of the living room not wanting to feel like I was just there to kiss ass or to try to make them like me. I started looking through some comic books in a bedroom when Tim walked in also looking around at the various stuff in Jonnies room. Being the lead singer as well as having a known past in the ska band Operation Ivy, he was the most popular in the Rancid clan and often the person most people tried to talk to. He asked if I was into comics and I said not really. He asked if I did anything besides being in a band, and I said that my friends are all in art school and they make movies and I help with that. I thought that would make me sound cool. As no one wants to be a lame punk rocker, you want to be a cool punk rocker. An indie film actor, I guess I could say that. I was feeling really cool about myself when he asked, "Well what movies have you been in lately?"

I thought to myself, shit, I just want to go back to being the shy guy who just laughed at everything they were saying. But now I was in a real life conversation and I didn't want to seem nerdy. I knew that he was thinking that maybe I was in some real indie movies (like some b-horror movie since it seemed the punk rockers always loved their low budget horror flicks), but I was only in student movies, and that is a big difference. My last role was the plumber in "Portrait of a Serial Plumber." A video done for kicks at my house that had maybe 5 student "actors" and was shown a few times at friends parties. One of the dumbest things I had ever done film wise. But, I couldn't seem like a dumbass in front of someone like Tim Armstrong. He was 90's punk royalty for crying out loud. So I quickly came up with what I thought would be a cool title and told him "I just finished working on my friends film called Cemetery Gates, it's like about the undead coming back and shit."

"Cool" he replied in his scratchy voice as he kept looking at various comics.

I then slinked back into the living room and disappeared into the laughter, ass kissing, and ball busting between bands.

At that time, Rancid was being contacted by the big major labels that were looking to cash in on the 1990's rebirth of punk music. In 1994, Green Day was breaking into the mainstream and everyone wanted a piece of this new reborn scene. A scene that now had plenty of young suburban kids spending their parents' money. We heard stories of labels including Madonna's own side record company taking them out to eat at expensive places. I thought what a sight that had to be. These Rancid punkers dressed in their leather jackets with metal studs and some suit and tie guy sitting across from them laughing at everything they said.

In South Carolina, The Bollweevils actually didn't make the same bill with Rancid, so they set up space for us a block away to play at an after show gig. The Rancid concert was packed and even though they mentioned our after show a few times during their set, no one really came to check us out. But half way into our little show, the Rancid boys came in and started a four-man mosh pit. It seemed like they were enjoying themselves and I was hoping it was taking them back to the days were they could go to a show and have fun and not have a hundred kids come up to them and ask if they were going to sign to a major label or not.

On another tour The Bollweevils took later on to the west coast, Rancid's drummer Bret somehow heard through word of mouth that my snare drum head broke. He made a few calls and he had a friend bring one to a show we did near his local town. Things like that showed me that maybe being popular and getting "famous" in the scene didn't have to ruin who you were as a person. You could be popular and remain nice as well. Further, after that show, Lars from Rancid came by and offered a place for us to stay. He shared some small house in the Bay area with some guys in the band Screw 32 I think.

And something I regret to this day, well two things...one being I left my favorite blue hoodie at his place (a good hoodie on the road can be a pillow, blanket, heck even your best friend at times) and the other being that Lars asked us Weevils to go to a party with him and we all declined. Who declines going to a party? Well, we did. We had a long drive the next day and were tired after our show. Being tired is not a rock and roll thing to be on a party night.

I personally was wide awake after showering as it seemed owning a hot water heater was not a punk thing to do. Something about freezing cold water running down your privates that will keep you alert for hours.

So we all crashed and in the early hours of the morning the party goers came back. I awoke on the floor and remember looking up at these sexy legs and wasn't sure if I was dreaming. As I looked up in a daze, this shoe comes straight down on my face. As I said "ouch", she told me she was sorry but she thought I was just a pile of clothes.

It was the most action I got on that whole tour.

But enough Rancid name-dropping tour stories, let's get back to busy summer of 1994.

With alternative and punk music becoming so popular, not all the shows could be held within our community and at smaller clubs. The Bollweevils decided to go against the opinion of the scene (more on that later) and play The Metro. This venue was viewed as the establishment, as it would host major label bands and had a history of not really caring about the local punk scene. Metro had hosted a few punk shows and we felt it was our turn to play one. We were booked to play July 8th 1994, and we asked our friends in 88 Fingers Louie (who were on the rise) to play. Joining us too would be the popular political Canadian punk rock band Propaghandi and another Chicago band called The Fighters. I was (and still am) a huge fan of Propagandhi's *How To Clean Everything* record and was eager awaiting meeting them and watching their set. Hours before the show, Propaghandi backed out as they learned that the Metro was a larger establishment that had some corporate sponsors and all that. They were known for staying away from anything that could be considered giving into the man or being too commercialized.

A friend from New Jersey and his band Hodge Podge just happened to be in town and sleeping on my floor, so they took the opening slot. The other two Chicago bands played before us. Outside a local punk girl who loved stirring things up handed out flyers for where Propagandhi would be playing and was calling out anyone lined up for our show to be sell outs. I remember being somewhat attracted to this girl, but with her crazy personality we obviously never really hit it off, other than her throwing water at me at the Fireside Bowl once. I guess somehow I had become the establishment. A poor person's establishment, but I was part of The Man. (On a side note a year or two later, like most extreme punks, she would eventually tone it down and become a normal person.) During the show the bouncers stayed off to the side. Maybe they thought it was better to leave everyone alone, as we asked if the club could not put up their big metal barricade and let us control the situation. Somehow with witnessing some crowd surfing during 88 Fingers Louie (remember in 1994 even though everyone was doing it, shit everyone is STILL doing it) the security guys really didn't know how to handle it all. By the time we took the stage the crowd and bouncers were not getting along and it was turning into a little pressure cooker. We launched into our set and towards the end the bouncers thought they had to claim the front of the stage. They had no idea of the type of band we were. It didn't matter to us who was on the stage and we didn't want any division between us and the crowd. This got to Daryl and Ken the most who then somehow seemed a little more upset. Daryl jumped into the crowd as he often did and I could tell the bouncers didn't really want to help him get back to the stage. As he flopped back onto the stage the crowd got really into it. Daryl then tried to pull back this HUGE bounce (picture a black Hulk but without those tiny purple shorts.) The bouncer slipped on the wet stage and I thought he was going to get up and punch Daryl to the moon, but the tension soon resolved as we were coming to the end of our set anyway. It would only build until the following year.

As we played places like Metro we started to really see not only our crowd growing in numbers but the whole popularity of the kind of music we were playing along with it. We were for sure leaving behind the days of only 10-20 people at our shows and growing and doing things differently. Don't get me wrong some of those early shows where we had to fight to get on the bill and then play our asses off so some would like us and others would give us a golf clap only helped build the band and make us appreciate everything that was coming our way. Some of those house shows also kept us honest.

I remember packing my stuff up after we played our set at a house show, and watching Los Crudos perform and take the intensity level higher in living room. Los Crudos was a Chicago hardcore band that sang in Spanish and talked about various social issues. They were nothing short of amazing to watch. Such intensity even if you didn't understand a words they were screaming. We welcomed the chance to play with any band, and certain times the other bands inspired us to be better. We always gave it our all, and that is something I can honestly say about both Bollweevils and Oblivion. That is part of the reason why both bands soon stopped playing shows together, even though it was easier on my schedule, it wasn't easy on my body to give 100% and then have to go up and do it again minutes later.

We now went from driving on the weekends as far as we could to play shows and race back to be home in time for our normal Monday-Friday boring life of school, work, school, work repeat, to now flying out to L.A. to do a one off show, meaning playing one night and then going home the next.

Bill asked us to come play the legendary Roxy in L.A., and on a Saturday of all things. Wow, a Saturday night on the Sunset Strip! Now that's rock and roll! My music dream was coming true. I would be at the same club where people like John Lennon and Keith Moon had drinks. Where bands like Ratt and Jane's Addiction played and where The Ramones filmed a concert scene for their cheesy movie "Rock N Roll High School." I realized my dream was really only partially coming true as I was still doing normal boring things like school and work. But soon, I thought, soon my life will change. I was sure I would bump into celebs and they would help me carry my drums into the club and then after the show we all would go off and party at some big mansion overlooking the Hollywood sign. Would I bang Uma or Winona first? Ah heck, it's always a free for all in Hollywood, we would for sure have a celebrity threesome. The whole flight there I looked out the window daydreaming and grinning ear to ear.

So now back to reality...Dr. Strange was doing a showcase of all the bands on the label with the great Riverside California ska-punk band, The Vodoo Glow Skulls, headlining at the Roxy.

We were mid bill out of the five band showcase, meaning bands played after and before us. The crowd was there which was nice. The first two bands played well, and then we took the stage with something to prove. We had put out our first full length record, *Stick your Neck Out,* and wanted to show people why these Chicago dorks deserved to be out here amongst the real bands. We stormed through our set stopping only once when the crowd seemed to get out of hand in the pit area. It's always you freaks in the pit. I remember a local kid telling Ken to play it safe as there might be gang involvement due to the makeup of the West Hollywood crowd.

Leaving the stage and helping break up a fight or two was something we saw Rancid do just months before on our short tour of the south. My opinion is that they aren't paying me enough to risk accidently taking an accidental punch from one big ass sweaty guy to another. I will just stop playing the drums and put my hands on my hips and give them a very stern look as to say, "now you big lugs stop that riff raff, so we can please get on with our set" which was of course full of songs provoking people to behave in such riff raff ways. After all, punk is rebellious.

As we left that historic stage and walked past the smoke filled backstage area filled with members of The Vodoo Glow Skulls lighting up, we knew we had just played our asses off and for sure showed why this little Chicago band deserved to be on a Californian record label.

Not to leave L.A. without some kind of hoopla, we tried to sell our merch (t-shirts and the such) outside as the guy inside was making the bands price up their cd's and shirts so that the club could get an outrageous cut from it. We made a lot of new fans that night and were having a blast hanging out with the people at the club, even with this manager guy being a dick about selling stuff. A few choice words were said and we went back to Docs place and closed out an amazing night that I will never forget.

Stick your Neck Out was filled with peppy punk tracks just like our 7 inches were. From "Dehumanize," "Happy," and

"John Doe" (Where Ken always loved screaming the count off to that song), to some mid tempo but still heavy songs like "The Failure of Bill Dozer." We even got to play our little tribute to a horrible horror movie we watched once or twice at Bob's called "Truth or Dare." And of course it was almost a rule that you had to put on some punked up version of an 80's pop song, our choice was Tommy Tutone's "Jenny 8675309." We all were very proud of putting together a release that we could be happy with and we hoped that our friends and fans would like it as well. It was getting good press in the punk scene and was gaining the attention of people who were looking for a new band to come out of Chicago, as the city at the time was gaining exposure in the national spotlight. We also caught the attention of Ford City Auto Parts because we borrowed their logo of a guy with a long neck for our cover. Their lawyers sent us a letter and we had to change some of the look of the guy, so that's why there are two slightly different versions of the cover.

The California band Offspring had a huge summertime hit that year. In my opinion it's one of their worst songs in "Come Out and Play," or more known as "Keep 'em Separated" tune. Their *Smash* disc had so many better songs including a nice cover of The Didjit's "Killboy Powerhead."

They had scheduled this October 17th show to be at the very nice Vic Theatre in Chicago. It held 1,400 people and that would be a lot more than the average show of 100-300 kids we were used to at the time. The Vic was where most of the alternative bands were playing. I had seen Jesus Jones, Jesus Lizard and a lot of other shows that had nothing to do with Jesus there. Most of the shows seemed to be over sold, and the medium sized Chicago clubs (Riv, Vic, Metro, even Aragon to a degree) at this point were for sure cashing in on any alternative music success they could. I was at more than a couple shows where you were crammed in so much that it was impossible to get both feet on the ground. You would alternate which foot you had flat on the floor and which was cramped up on another person's shoe in the pit area. So due to the Bollweevils' new relationship with Rancid and their booker Stormy, we were asked to open the three band bill, but it was just listed as Rancid and Offspring. This would be our first big show full of the regular kids. Meaning that the punk kids who once liked these bands would be staying at home and all the cool clean shopping mall type kids would be there. I thought that I would have to get used to this if I wanted to be a big time rocker, as you just can't play in front of your friends or people you fit in with and make it.

I saw this as a great opportunity to try to talk to people about our local punk scene and what we were all about. So young and naive back then I was. I made this one page flyer that listed all the punk shows, clubs, stores that people that were interested in the scene could check out. In hopes that if anyone gave a shit about the real local punk scene, they would know where to go and whom to support.

So the big show comes around and we got a 25 minute set time and it was the first time were we got backstage food and treated like little rock stars. Well, Offspring actually had the food, but once they left to do sound check it was our duty to quickly go in grab some tasteless pasta and run out before they all came back. After our sound check we left our stuff and walked off the stage. I remember trying to get a pair of my drum sticks out of my bag and having a big Chicago-type union guy tell me "don't you dare go out on that stage." Union rules forbid us to even look at the stage until our set time, but I told him I was a Teamster member myself (as I was still throwing boxes around at UPS nightly), but he looked at me like I was joking. He probably thought my skinny punk ass never saw an honest hard day's work. Oh well, silly union rules.

We walked outside to see all the kids lined up. It was a lot bigger line than we had ever seen. We knew hardly anyone in that line. It was for sure a very different crowd then was coming to our local punk shows. A cleaner, more suburban type of punk if you will.

I remember walking to the stage from the back stage area and there is a turn before you go up to the side stage area where you come close to the audience, and some people actually reached out to touch us. This was when all you had was a chance to reach out and touch someone, as taking any kind of photo or selfie with a rocker was non-existent by decades. I thought to myself, these poor kids think we are Rancid, they will feel dumb when we take the stage and they found out we are only the stupid local opening band. Oh well, it was nice to get touched anyway—it was definitely a rock and roll ego moment to have people reaching for you. One part creepy, one part cool.

We took the stage and Daryl did his usual excellent job in communicating with the audience and breaking down that band/crowd barrier (but not that actual dumb barricades they had up which took away like 20% of the main floor space up front). Shows like that to me always went by really quick, and your playing is on autopilot and you go into this outer body experience. I never felt the intimacy or realness that came over me playing at a smaller club or house show.

After our set I walked up to the balcony area to hand out my flyers I made about various "punk" things, and more than one person was surprised that someone from the band was walking amongst them. From that point on I knew that when I went to see bands even at these "bigger" shows, that the opening bands could be just as broke as me. Not everyone was a rock star.

We rode on the success of that show right into the next month where local punk gods Pegboy asked us to play before them at their Thanksgiving eve show also held at the Vic Theatre. I was now entering a time in the fall of 1994 when school and work were being left in the dust in importance, as the demands on my time were outrageous. Oblivion was going full steam, I was playing in a tribute band KISSS, Bollweevils were exploding with all these larger venue shows, I was writing music reviews and articles for various publications, and all the while I was still searching for a girlfriend.

We were the second band on and more than did our job with warming up the Chicago crowd before Pegboy hit the stage. It was a different crowd than we saw the month before at the Vic, as this was more of a Chicago blue collar, slightly older drunk punk crowd. We were a solid band from playing all the shows as well as we still practiced weekly in my basement. We had recorded a lot of songs and Dr. Strange records put them on a compilation History of The Bollweevils Part 1.

I already felt old as I was now 23 and most of the kids at the shows were 16-19. I assumed this rock star thing should happen before I reached 25 so I could enjoy it in my youth. To have a CD come out about your "history" made me realize how fast time flies. Especially in the young and fast paced punk scene. We closed off 1994 as weekend warriors driving down to return to Knoxville Tennessee this time to play a New Year's Eve show at the Mercury Theatre. Our van would break down coming home after the show and it was the first time I had to take a Greyhound. Looking at a map I figured I had a straight shot from where our van broke down in Kentucky to Chicago. But nooooo, Greyhound buses have this ability to stop off at strange locations making your journey go on and on, taking twice as long. There's a reason why those people look the way they do on the bus. It was miserable. But my year was only just getting started.

1995 was a crazy year for me and the Weevils. Club Foot (a Chicago punk rock bar) opened and on top of all my other non-school, non-work activities, I was now DJ'ing weekly on Tuesday nights as the weekends were filled with venturing out as far as we could to play shows in nearby states like Michigan, Tennessee and Iowa to name a few. We found ourselves back in

Indiana to record our second record *Heavyweight* again at Sonic Iguana Studios. Even though we had recorded off and on all year for various songs for compilations, we knew that this batch of songs had to hold some weight as even in the punk scene you always had talk of the sophomore jinx. Meaning you had a whole career and childhood angst to build up on for your first full record, and now the second will be done in a lot shorter time. It is thought that a band's second record usually sucks compared to their first. I have seen that, but just as many bands put out awesome second records as well and third records and so on. Since our first record was mostly received very well in the local and national reviews we got from the various music 'zines at the time, we didn't want to disappoint the Doc, our friends and fans, and of course ourselves.

We recorded and mixed it all in two and a half days. We seemed to play shows and record at break neck speeds. Daryl's vocals were spot on, Ken's guitar was loud and chunky and Bob and I continued to keep the rhythms as fast but yet still melodic as our little fingers would allow us. Looking back now I still think like our first record, that it still sounds fresh and furious. After hearing a quote from some burnt out kid we videotaped on tour, the record starts with "Twenty Something," "Fence Sitter," and "Last Laugh" at break neck speed. One of my favorite little snare drum parts is in the middle of "Last Laugh." I was taking all my sexual frustrations out in that one. The lyrics to "Major Problems" explained how we all felt about the rising popularity of the punk scene and some of the bands going over to major labels leaving the independent "do it yourself" ethics behind. We had Jason from The Fighters shoot a video around Chicago for "Fence Sitter" as we were asked to submit something for a punk video compilation but didn't want to do a standard band at show with crazy crowd video. As we waited for the release of the record we appeared on many compilations.

We also found ourselves headlining the Metro again on April 22nd this time we knew we could draw a good local crowd and wanted them to be exposed to some of our favorite out of state bands like Boris the Sprinkler from Wisconsin and Sinkhole from the east coast.

Boris was a band lead by the crazy front man Rev. Norb who had a column in the punk fanzine MRR as well as was a known wacky person in the scene. Boris put on an amazing show with songs filled with a sense of humor like "(Do You Wanna) Grilled Cheese." The scene needed Norb and his antler helmet badly as it often took itself way too seriously.

To add to my schedule The Bollweevils had learned a lot of Naked Raygun covers during multiple practices and performed them as the cover band "Rat Patrol" for a Memorial Day Concert at the Fireside Bowl. A now legendary Chicago bowling alley that hosted some of the best punk shows of the mid to late 90's. Pierre Kezdy, the bass player for Naked Raygun, joined us for a few songs and it was amazing. We got good reactions for our songs, but you play Raygun for a Chicago crowd and you can see the intensity go to another level. I could only imagine what it must be like to actually be in the real band. It was after the show I noticed that Raygun's drummer Eric Spicer was also at the show. I wish I had known because I would have gladly given up my drum set and rocked out on tambourine or something to "I Don't Know."

In this crazy time crunch I had to once again do the rock star thing and take a plane to a show. In June 1995, Daryl and I flew out to California and met Bob, Ken, and our van. They were there with some other Chicago friends who would help sell merchandise and keep us company on the road. This was the start of a crazy tour with the White Kaps who were a long running surf punk band.

We were promoting our *Heavyweight* record/cd (which also came out on picture disc, my first and only picture disc). After landing in California, we played at the Showcase Theatre in Corona and since Dr. Strange was well known in this parts, the show had a great turnout. From that point on we played pretty much a show a night heading back east home to Chicago. We noticed even in places like Nevada (where we played with A.F.I. who was just starting to break big into the scene) and Arizona where we hadn't played before we were getting great crowds. After the Nevada show to celebrate Ken and I walked around town feeling pretty good about ourselves and wanted to do the Motley Crue rock star thing and hang with some strippers. We soon found ourselves in a club. The most darkly lit strip club I have ever seen. We kept knocking into chairs as we tried to find a nice place to sit. We soon realized we were pretty much the only two guys there. You know you are in a classy strip club when you can see strollers lined up just off stage as not every working mommy can find a babysitter, ya' know. So this woman comes over and ask us if we want to dance, and at this point we both were wanting to leave and forget our strip club idea. A big bouncer comes over and tells us we would like a dance, so we get one and I think I was more attracted to Ken then this dancer whose best days were probably 20 or so years ago. We both left pretty fast after that and went back to the area where all the punks were hanging out after the show. I was hearing talk about how this other band that came through town recently Blink 182 was loved and hated amongst the pop punk fans. I knew of them as their video was on some VHS compilation that The Bollweevils were a part of. It would be just a few years later when this Blink band would replace Green Day as America's biggest "punk" band. Again, so close to my dream but yet so far away.

The move to go on Dr. Strange had proven good choice as the distribution of our record and CD's were slowly getting around the states. One cool keepsake I got around then was a copy of our first CD with its Japanese labeling from J!MCO Records. I thought: if I ever want to tour full time and see places like Japan, I would for sure have to leave my work and school behind. With the way that both bands were growing, it didn't seem like too much of a dumb choice, but times would soon get strange.

To finish that tour we had a big *Heavyweight* record release at the Metro on July 4th once again in front of a crazy crowd. We would record the show for our next release "Weevil live" with Rob Roy from the Underdog Records group doing the sound production that night. There was drama outside before the show as we had set it up so that our touring friends in Doc Hopper and White Kaps would play in the middle and another band Horace Pinker opening. Some of the guys in Horace were upset that they had to play first when they thought they were a little above that at the time. Ah the drama, and that drama didn't take long to hit the stage as the security guards vs the crowd thing started to take hold again. When Daryl thought one of his friends got kicked out (we later found out he only was escorted off the stage and then went downstairs to catch some air) we stopped playing. After we realized that there were a lot of pumped up people to see us play, we kicked into another song which erupted into the crowd including a lot of our friends coming up on stage to try to jump off before the bouncers go to them. Punks against Jocks at its best—or so it seemed.

Everything went from playing a fast song in rock and roll dreamland to slow pace real life. On my left I saw Ken slowly wind up to throw a punch (almost pro wrestling style) to a bouncer who was helping push the audience off, and to my right I saw more kids rushing the stage that was now full of big security dudes. It was a mess. I walked from behind my drums and tried to calm people down and tell them to get off the stage so we could possibly go back to finishing our set. As Daryl, Ken, the show promoter, and bouncers were settling things, I remember sitting on the drum platform with Bob and tossing my sticks into the crowd in frustration of it all. One of the guys from The White Kaps said it perfectly into the microphone: "Let the kids have fun, assholes." It seemed that punk rock was still a little dangerous. Just as quickly as everything went a little crazy it all calmed down and as soon as I found another pair of sticks we completed our set.

It was after the show that we said we wouldn't play Metro again and also rumors that we were banned from there, but neither really seemed to be true. Even with all that action I think it wasn't our best show from that time period, but I was still glad to be there. I would say I was glad to be on the record, but check the record cover...I guess I should have known I was out soon after that one eh? It was a dick move and sucked, but throughout the years I have known band members to get the boot in many odd fashions from having their gear thrown out in front of their residences (often while the van is still moving) to having one member bang their girlfriend. So in all, I guess a phone call wasn't too bad. At least it wasn't collect.

So about that call...

The summer was hectic. A month after Oblivion took off for 10 days in to go to the east coast, the Bollweevils also went east for a five day extended weekend. I was now out of all my time asking off from work. The Bollweevil's short east coast tour in September 1995 would end up being my last tour with them. At the time we were all getting along great and talking about what we would do next. Daryl's medical training was getting intense, but Bob, Ken and I couldn't stop talking about touring more in support of our *Heavyweight* record. Friendship mixed with business was hard. Like it or not when your band starts putting out records and touring you do have to look at it like a business to some degree. Our friendships were always at the heart of the band, but we all were worrying about our futures. I wasn't aware how close I would be to not having to worry about any future and not just with The Bollweevils but with life itself.

After some Boston shows we loaded up and decided to drive overnight to get to Philly early for a small afternoon show. I got behind the wheel and said I would do the whole thing so the guys could rest. Even though it was only a five and a half hour drive, I was exhausted from the start after the show.

Somewhere just over the halfway point in New York I started fading. I remember looking down for any pop (yeah, I say pop) to drink to help me stay alert. I downed all I could find and noticed all my bandmates were passed out. Even Bob who was riding copilot. The copilot was usually there to also keep the driver awake on tour, but I might have told him I got this one short five-hour drive no problem. I started to notice the taillights on the van in front of us driven by the Doc Hopper guys starting to fade off. It was at this time I remembered how Daryl told us he would see t-shirts dancing along the roadside when his exhaustion was setting in from driving. I was not seeing shirts, but rather the cast of Bozo Circus and Planet of the Apes hanging out in the road. As I swerved to avoid them I dozed off. 100 percent asleep. In dreamland I head a trombone and then a trumpet, or...no wait, was it a horn? A VAN HORN!

My heart raced as I awoke and saw that our van was just a foot away from hitting the center rail dividing highway 95. I got the van straightened out and was now fully awake and bright eyed which was good as it was soon time to start paying some tolls.

As I finally pulled off into a rest stop to relieve my full bladder, The Doc Hopper guys told me what they saw. I had drifted to the far right lane from the center and then back to the far left again. The guys in their van thought I was jerking around trying to either be funny or signal to them that I wanted to pull off to a rest stop soon. When I again went all the way to the right lane again and then raced to the far left, they knew something was up and honked their horns. They told me I had a sea of vehicles behind me all afraid to pass this swerving van.

I was glad no one was injured as people die that way just as they do from drunk drivers. From that point on, I would come up with all sort of silly ways to keep myself awake behind the wheel.

Back home the Bollweevils had a show at the most popular place to play in Chicago at the time, The Fireside Bowl. What once was a dirty bowling alley that some punks decided to host a few shows at, quickly became the place to play for many indie and up and coming rock bands. They even received national exposure and the bartenders and bookers all became little celebrities in the local scene. Bollweevils loved the smelly intimacy of it, and we got to keep a lot of the door money to divide between us and the other bands almost equally as we always tried to give more to the touring bands no matter who headlined the show.

We played a show at the Fireside Bowl Sunday October 8th that featured the Bouncing Souls. We played before them, but some of the crowd actually left after us and missed a great show. I had no idea it would be the last time I would play a Chicago show as a Bollweevil. Two weeks later I drove up for a gig just over the Illinois border in Kenosha, Wisconsin. After the small show, while I was driving home the singer of Urban DK (who also played that night) he asked me how I liked being in the Bollweevils, saying that it had to be fun getting so popular. I remarked to him that I didn't like how sometimes the Weevils seemed to try to have a tough guy or street image, (even though I did once pick up Ken who was busted over a traffic stop at Cook County jail, so I guess in some way that lend some street cred to Ken but not the whole band) but that overall I loved being in two different bands. Plus, I had just quit my UPS job to be able to allow more time for both bands. I was worried not to have a pay check and insurance and all, but I just felt like both bands needed my time and if I was going to take things to the next level to make my dream come true, I had to do it.

A week later as I loaded up my gear after an Oblivion Elmhurst VFW show (the place that you always had a chance of seeing a decapitation, as ceiling fans and crowd surfing don't mix) I again mentioned to Bob that I would be gone for six weeks on tour with Oblivion, he mentioned he thought it was four and now that it is six it really puts a strain on the band. I told him that the day I get home, I would be up for practicing and playing some December shows. Fast forward a few days and I find myself in Mark Piss place in Pennsylvania (the guy who drew the artwork for history of part 1 and 2) and before we leave for the Oblivion gig he says Daryl is on the phone for me. Daryl in a few words tells me I am out of the band as they thought I would never quit, but how could I have time to do both bands and that they were going to do another Rat Patrol (The Naked Raygun cover thing we did) show with CJ from the Fighters on drums and then get another drummer for the Bollweevils. I was totally devastated.

Ever get that punched in the stomach when someone you care about breaks up with you? Well, I got the fist to the tummy all right. That night Scott sand Pete told me I would be ok, but yup, it hurt real bad. To this day I don't think they fully understand or care why. It was not just not being able to play drums behind them anymore, it was getting a phone call from friends telling you, you are out. How could I not take it personal on so many levels? I only recently quit my job due to being in two bands. By leaving my "real job" I thought I would be free when either band wanted to play, practice, record and tour. With just being in one local trying to be national band, I knew it was a death wish, but maybe with being in two bands on that level, I could somehow pull off this wacky musician dream thing.

I also thought that after four long years, we were solid friends, not just people you could replace in a heartbeat. Looking back now, I am sure they didn't do it to hurt me as a friend, but in their mind it was in the best interest of the band was to get a drummer that was only in their band, and not splitting up their time. It most likely was Ken's choice to do what was best for his band and not an individual member. But at that time, Daryl needed time to do things for med school, and I needed time for Oblivion, but drummers are easily the most replaceable as no one even notices us half the time. I knew I should have learned to play the damn guitar. I also thought, could it be something petty like my kick drum skills or lack thereof?

As I remember they always wanted the Fat Wreck Chords sound, and even had Dom from 88 Fingers Louie talk to me the year before while waiting to play at Lucy's Record Shop in Nashville. They told him to teach me some kick drum techniques. I always had good enough hands, but my kick drum skills were I guess lacking. Punk rock was easy enough to play and is supposed to be fun. But of course it helps to have some kind of skill at your instrument. I blame jazz band back in high school. Our instructor didn't like any kick drum in his jazz. I would play a whole concert with only using the kick peddle as a foot rest. So somehow when I started to play faster punk songs I always managed this strange heart beat pattern on the kick and was fine with that as I could spend more time working on good fills, or patterns, like the neat-o 16 note pattern on the high-hat for "999-Stoney." Was jazz the reason why I was out of a punk band?

But that kick wouldn't be the last blow.

I came back to Chicago and would see the guys around town. Sometime later (I think in all my time away I only caught one Weevils show without me) Oblivion played with them in Elgin. I didn't like how they sounded that night, but watched on from the t-shirt selling area. By the way what is it with t-shirts? People will buy them more than your own music. And some punk bands look like they are bringing a damn clothing store on the road with them. I had a few people during their set tell me they wish I was still in the band, but all I could do was nod and smile.

I didn't watch too much as it felt like watching some new dude sleeping with your girlfriend in a way, except different cause they were all dudes on stage, but anyway...after the show I gave Daryl a ride home. We didn't really talk about the Weevils, as there was nothing to say. I was just glad to be able to show that I was still a friend even though we weren't bandmates anymore. Daryl and I got back together on stage at the Fireside soon after that to play a Bollweevils song at the request of a touring band called Co-Ed from California. It made their day to have us join them, and to be honest I was all smiles as I played through the song to the small but happy crowd.

Also around that time I worked at a daycare with Ken Weevil's girlfriend at the time Nikki. Touring with Oblivion was not making ends meet (or frozen pizza) which you will read soon. Nikki was cute so I didn't mind talking with her to find out how the guys were doing from time to time. And it sure beat actually paying attention to the unruly kids I was supposed to be watching on the playground.

I heard from her that the band was considering calling it quits.

I remember meeting Brett (from Houseboy who took over my Bollweevil drumming duties) while sitting at the Fireside Bowl. I should have known as the spring before I got the axe in fall 1995, Bob and Ken had him come out to a show to watch me play. And I thought he just wanted some pointers on how to twirl sticks. Brett and I drank and laughed over various gig stories and also talked about the different personalities of the band. It was shortly after that that I sat and found myself having beers with Ken. One night sitting at the Fireside Bowl's bar, he told me the Weevils were indeed thinking about calling it quits after a final tour and asked if I would be interested in playing on it. It was the closest I would hear of an apology for how my exit was handled so I told Scott and Pete Oblivion (who both looked at me like I was going off to sleep with a psycho ex-girlfriend) that I would need two weeks off from doing anything with Oblivion to do this final Bollweevils tour.

I was excited, as I wanted to end on a high note and show whatever audience in whatever city we played what we were all about. Well, fast forward a few weeks later and I again was at the Fireside Bowl (I served drinks there from time to time for money, I wasn't a drunk) hanging out. Ken came up to me and said they didn't want to upset Brett (fuck my feelings I guess) and that the final tour would be without me. Enter punch to the stomach feeling yet again. From what I heard it wasn't that great anyway with Bob handling vocals towards the end of the tour and lots of drama and strain on the friendships. I was asked to write a short piece on my time in the Weevils for *History of the Bollweevils Part 2* (Dr Strange Records) which was supposed to be their final release. I turned my paper in to Ken and wasn't that surprised when they didn't include it in the booklet.

When Oblivion was with Dr Strange Records and promoting our soon to be split CD with Man Dingo we were told we could join a Dr. Strange label tour in the summer of 1997. It had the Dr. Strange bands Whatever, and Ken Weevil's new thing The Feds.

Years ago, I went into detail in the late great Underdog Zine about the incident where Ken pushed me hard into the back of the Oblivion van as I was loading up my drums after show in Penn. He didn't like Oblivion playing the intro to the Weevils song "Dehumanize." Shit, I was the one with the idea to play that intro part after the end of each verse anyway (the slow countdown part was originally only in the beginning), so it is like .08% my song anyway. All I could do was laugh at the incident as I really didn't want to fight. It takes a lot to get me to that point. And I sure didn't think a mad and drunk Kenny was worth it by any means. The parking lot already had some dumb ass kids fighting and cops were on the way. The last thing I wanted to do was to add to that drama and make it so no traveling punk bands could ever play that club again. In the article I wrote however, I did challenge him to a boxing match at the Fireside Bowl with money going to a charity. I was thinking to either Food Not Bombs or Hardcore Against Hunger at the time. I thought it would have been funny, and I really wanted to put the gloves on along with some Apollo Creed type America boxing shorts and robe. But to this day I am not sure if Ken ever read my article anyway.

And of course with all the new reunion shows and band activities I wasn't included as they have moved on and never looked back. The first reunion was interesting. I was sent an email on how it would be awesome for The Bollweevils classic line up to get back together for this radio benefit. I was excited to come up from Florida and be able to play again with those guys. But it seemed from the start that things were off. And from various emails from the guys it seemed that they would like me to do just the encore. I took it as an insult as they didn't think I could relearn the songs in time and that I would fly up a few days early to get a practice or two in. I knew I could easily learn 12-14 tunes and play them, but it was obviously more to it than that. We were on separate pages. I thought it would be cool, and finally a way to feel appreciated for all I did for the band in my four years. The years that produced the best Bollweevil music by far. I was pissed, but it seemed they already had another drummer they had in mind for the show anyway. Silly me to think I would play drums at a reunion anyway? Since that show they have done Riot Fest and other gigs, and to be honest I wish things ended differently and were different with me and them, but in life you don't always get want you want. It's all murky water under the punk bridge I guess. You just have to smile, wish everyone the best, and say thanks for the memories.

"The critic knows you're wrong!" -No Empathy

All along while playing in bands in the 90's I wrote for
various entertainment publications. I thought it would be
simple. I would be a rock star, and then all my friends would be
rock stars and I would write about them and become like a
famous writer and stuff. Simple. And if I didn't become a star,
well then I could still do my writings and stay on the road. I
never thought I liked writing until I noticed that in some of my
High School English classes were where I got some of my best
grades. I never had any plans for my future other than playing
in bands, so when other kids in school knew why they wanted
to go to college, I would be envious. So after High School
ended, I signed up to work nights throwing packages around at
UPS, and in the day time I went to the local junior college,
Triton College in River Grove Illinois. Since English and music
were the only things that somewhat interested me I thought
what the heck, I will write music articles for the school paper as
a music critic. I chose to write about punk and alternative
music since metal was still the flavor of the year in many jaded
journalist eyes and I wanted to be a little different. And also
cause I knew bands like Screeching Weasel would offer more
listening enjoyment then getting demos from crappy local hair
bands that were still holding onto the dream of making it. I was
still on the "street team" for the local metal station WVVX,
which just meant I got some free stickers and concert passes,
the highlight of it all was going to see a greatly underrated L.A.
rock/metal band at the time called LOVE/HATE for free. 1990
was when the alternative storm was coming from the west and
metal bands were on their way out no matter if they cut their

hair or not, no matter how the big record executives tried to keep their boys famous.

A local College DJ would have me on his show sometimes to talk about my music reviews which were actually being read by some of the students. I even won some cheesy Junior College journalist award downstate for my article on the Chicago band Pegboy. I would sit there give my opinions on music like it meant anything, oh wait that's what this book is about, so yeah for sure it means something! I was told one review of the local Chicago metal band Cutlass pissed some of the band members, and he asked me on air if reviewing bands would be an unhealthy habit. I just pictured walking out to my car and getting the shit beat out of me by some dudes in leather pants and more hair spray to kill every damn polar bear on this planet. It would serve my opinionated ass right. I soon found I wasn't alone not only was I bored with most local rock and metal music and looking to the punk and alternative scenes for better sounds, but soon also most college kids would be doing the same.

One of my music reviews on Screeching Weasel caught the eye of one Joey Vindictive (I just love punk names) who wrote to me via the school paper address and sent me his first two seven inches. I brought them home and plopped them down on to my turntable and heard that trademark snarly snotty vocals and punchy guitars. He included a note that stated that he was glad someone in the school had good ears. I was glad to get some quality music for free. I spoke with Joey a few times on the phone about featuring other bands, and once when he called he asked if I knew any guitar players. I always wanted to be one myself, but the first available guitar player that came to mind was Pete Oblivion's and my friend, Billy Blastoff. Bill was playing with Pete in a side band of sorts called Amish Vomit, but I knew he wanted to do something more. After Bill joined them, Oblivion who was still mostly on the outside of the punk scene looking in, set up a few shows with The Vindictives. This writing was not only giving me an "in" to some cool local music, but it also giving me an "in" to a somewhat secretive world of the local punk scene. An "in" that would find me soon coming home from school and having my clueless and unimpressed mom telling me a "Mr. Weasel called" or a "Joey Queer" and also on another day a "Daniel Vappy" (Dan Vapid) called. I called back the number my mom wrote on a piece of paper and asking for Daniel and having the uncertain voice answer back "Daniel? Well this is Dan."

I was nervous to make a dork out of myself as to me these guys were the people I wanted to be like. Someone like Dan who played in bands like Sludgeworth and Screeching Weasel, bands that people actually gave a shit about. Most calls were either asking me to review something or even inviting me to ask either Bollweevils or Oblivion to open a show. They would say things like "hey can your band open up for this band at this show," and I would be all too happy to reply "Yes, for sure" and then after hanging up trying to figure out not only how I was going to fit the show into my school/work schedule, but also trying to figure out which band they wanted.

It was hard getting anyone out to shows in the early 90's scene for us unknown bands. In early 1993, Ben had Adam from Jawbreaker (one of the best bands ever to come out of California) called me and asked about where would be good place to play in the Chicago area since McGregors was no longer, and also that if the Bollweevils could play as well. I knew this writing habit of mine could bring good things, and I was excited to continue it even when my schedule was full with double band duties.

Ben Weasel also had asked me to do a scene report for his Panic Button 'zine. He basically told me he didn't go to shows anymore but he wanted to include some kind of Chicago punk scene report in his next 'zine. I had read Ben's articles in *Maximumrocknroll* (MRR) for some time now, I took this responsibility to heart...little ole me, being asked to give my two cents about the scene. I was also scared that if I messed it up, he would use me as something to discuss in his monthly column, so I didn't want to fuck up my writing homework. I quickly wrote a report up one up and dropped it off. It was always a two for one deal with Ben and Joey since at the time they lived in the same building. I remember going to the apartment building and looking at the names. None of the buzzers had their punk names on it...shit. I had to think hard about what their real last names were. I knew Ben would be home because his agoraphobia at the time was keeping him in a lot. I pictured him looking out, thinking what is this ass doing at my door looking around, and why doesn't he know how to press a button? Not really ever being accepted into any sort of clique in high school. I was over worried about not making a fool out of myself in front of the punk crowd. I would soon lose that fear not only in my writing but on stage as well.

So yup, this band reviewing stuff was not only fun for me and provided some free records, but it was also allowing me to open for bands that were breaking through in the scene. Those early shows opening for the bigger bands like Screeching Weasel, and Jawbreaker certainly helped expose the Bollweevils. For some reason Oblivion was off in its own direction and never was really asked to open that much in our early punk career. It was fine with me to have two bands doing separate things and drawing somewhat different crowds. Variety is the spice of life.

In 1993, when both bands were in full swing playing shows and recording for various 7 inches, I went over to U.I.C. (with my big bad associate of arts degree from Triton Junior College). I did a few music reviews including a review of No Empathy until the people at the paper got all jealous of how I had an "in" on the local rock scene. The local scene was finally getting some attention due to the success of Chicago acts like Smashing Pumpkins and Liz Phair. I didn't need any crap with trying to compete for space in the school paper now that everyone wanted to write about the alternative scene, so I went to writing for non-school associated publications like *Pop Smear* from NYC and *Subculture* based in Chicago. I just wanted to review my friends' bands and try to give them some exposure, but the magazines sometimes had other ideas. Once they sent me out to interview this up-and-coming alternative band called Supreme Love Gods who were playing at the Riv with Ned's Atomic Dustbin. I was sort of excited to see the Riv's backstage area as I really wanted to play their someday more than any other place in Chicago. I had to write a good article because if I succeeded I was told I would become the 'punk and alternative guy' and get my own my own column in which I could discuss anything I wanted to.

I walked through the back stage area and looked around and found a road manager who set me up with all the back stage passes I needed. As I looked around I noticed it didn't seem like a rock and roll crazy back stage party, but rather a bunch of homeless looking dudes setting up a bunch of chords and some tech guy hitting the drum set a million times over. Everyone looked tired and burnt out, but heck I didn't want to be some roadie, I wanted to be a rocker. I asked where the band was and they pointed up to this very tiny room. It was not the big backstage fiesta I thought it was going to be. I shook hands with the band members who all seemed nice enough and placed my little tape recorder at their feet. It was then that I wished I had actually listened to their CD. The promo disc had a sticker with labeling one song for the radio stations to play and I sort of played that song on my CD player, but I really didn't pay attention to it. I started off with my first big hard hitting question that came to mind...

"So how do you guys like being here in America?"

I got blank stares, my interview was starting off bad.

"Um, we're from California".

"Yeah umm right" (I was doing my best to recover),

"I meant how do you guys like touring with Neds in America, cause they're British and stuff?"

From there I mustered up maybe three or four more lame-ass questions and then walked around. At this time the crowd was let in so I hung out in the lobby hoping some cool alternative girl would see my passes and mistake me for one the guys in the band. Everyone walked right by me.

I went up to the balcony and watched the show and wrote down a few notes. The camera I brought sucked and even though the paper couldn't use any of my pictures. They did print the article and I was eventually given my own space to talk about anything I wanted to. It was fun getting into a show for free, but bands want to meet groupies or find out where to party. They really don't want to talk to some pimply-faced dork backstage, especially ones that don't even know what country they're from.

I kept getting more chances to write reviews and I even did the cheesy thing some D.J's and journalists do where I emceed a show. At least mine wasn't at some lame show it was a local punk rock night back at the Thirsty Whale that I set up. It featured some punk bands like the Hitmen and Raunchous Brothers who had the one and only front man Buck whose brother Dennis I knew well from singing in 88 Fingers Louie. It was strange to return to The Whale, a bad metal club that I thought I would never return to. The highlight of the night was listening to the Raunchous Brothers sing "Cock Rocker in the mall, leave me alone, I'm just trying to use, the fucking pay phone."

Such deep lyrics at a club that just years before was filled to the rim with cock rockers. Raunchous looked up to sexist bands like the Mentors, and at the time they were comical. Buck aka The Whipping Bastard, once told me I was the only member of the Bollweevils that didn't deserve a slug to the head. My love of metal I guess saved me in his thinking that the Weevils stood for everything wrong with punk music. Later in the 90's their anti pc lyrics became a little too much and one can only hope it's all a bad joke in the end.

I missed out on the chance to interview GWAR since Oblivion was late coming back from a weekend of shows in Canada, but I did get to interview some bands like this metal band called Buzzoven. People were usually nice over the phone and happy to get any kind of press they could. My local column was nice but when I started to write for national glossy publications like *PopSmear*, I felt like I was on my way to one day writing for Rolling Stone or I would for sure settle for the Illinois Entertainer. *PopSmear* was where I got to do video game reviews and use swear words in print. How damn cool I was. Where else could you read about Playstation's Pitfall *fucking* Harry. Watch out Hunter S. Thompson, here I come.

I also started my own small 'zine called B.O. which stood for Beyond Oblivion. I loved reading the diary and traveling type zines out there like *Dishwasher*, *Tales of Blarg* and *Cometbus* and wanted to do something similar. I wanted to show people I was so much more than some dumbass punk drummer. I could have my own opinions and write tour blogs and review all sorts of junk. But doing a quality 'zine takes time and that I didn't really have much of. So I only did three issues and left the 'zine writing to the pros. After that I wanted to start my own record label, and the first band I wanted to "sign" was this brand new band called Slapstick. I had known their singer Brendan for a while, since he was a fan of Oblivion's from the early days. Slapstick would eventually become one of Chicago's biggest bands, so maybe I should have tried to start a label. But with the little free time I did have in between bands, I kept on writing.

My main reason for spending so much time reviewing music and writing articles was that I was trying to build up the local scene and expose it a little more to the college kids. So many of the punk shows had plenty of young kids 16-19 year olds, but it seemed we seldom were able to capture the college kids and of course the hard to get 21 and over crowd. At that time they were at clubs like Lounge Ax or Avalon when the larger national acts on major labels or larger indie labels came through.

I still knew the press had some power to it. One of the best things from my reviewing came when the local Chicago publication Subculture magazine trusted anything I wrote. I would DJ with and book shows with Brian Peterson, and we came up with an idea to see how far we could take a fake band. We gave this band the name Craphole and he would list it on several flyers for places like Fireside Bowl where he booked shows. I think he even got the band listed on a Metro gig. I quickly wrote up a review for the bands demo and had it published, along with a show review. Our joke to life when some kid asked another who was at a Fireside Bowl show with Craphole listed on it how the opening band Craphole was? And the kid (maybe afraid to look uncool for missing the opening act, which never existed anyway) told him that the band kicked ass.

I am sure if we went ahead with our idea to sell the band's shirts at the show we would have sold a couple for sure. Never underestimate the written word I guess. We felt obligated to maybe form this band after all and we actually held a single practice for it. I was on drums, and Brian joined by Matt (who would soon make better music with his real band Alkaline Trio) played the guitar. We decided to leave the band idea be and we stuck the name on a few more flyers and our little dumb inside joke always gave us a giggle or two as we hung out.

From the mid 1990's to the early 2000's (even after Oblivion folded and I moved to Tampa) I wrote for Punk Planet. It's kind of like a lesser known *Maximumrocknroll*, but still a magazine that had its fair share of readers. Oblivion played several benefit shows (meaning the bands get nothing but a nice handshake) that went towards some dream of owning a building where all these punks could live together and have an art studio, bakery, performance club, and heck why not ever toss in some tennis courts. But the collective never took off, and I think they used the money saved to launch this new magazine. I soon found my mailbox was filled with 7 inches and CD's from bands (mostly crappy) from all over the world. At first I wanted to impress the staff at Punk Planet so I wrote s short story and reviewed 'zines and music and asked to do as much as possible. I would spend a lot of time on my reviews trying to show my skills as a writer. I would use honesty even if it meant saying it in a non -PC way. Several bands contacted the magazine and I took pride in that I was the most hated reviewer on the magazines staff (it took a few published letters to the editor to claim that throne).

They claimed me to be everything from sexiest, to well, I guess sexiest. But in a Spinal Tap way there is such a fine line between sexy and sexiest, and in the ultra-self-righteousness punk community back then, that line was really thin. Still bands would request that I review them, so it meant someone was still reading my reviews.

In the later years after I left Oblivion, I got bored and would use the review space to talk about wrestling and girls. To be truthful those last two years I spent reviewing, I was in Florida in a broken down trailer living in an animal sanctuary. I wasn't really listening to the bands other than a quick CD scan of their first three songs. I would toss any crap from the promo kits into the trash. I was burnt out. There were times of glory though when hearing new bands that would eventually become bigger like Coheed and Cambria, Flogging Molly, and unknown bands like The Sovietts from Minnesota, and Milloy from the UK somehow broke through my jaded mind and made me interested in music again. There was some very good stuff out there. And I also felt guilty for leaving the scene so to speak, and at times I would write email to various bands asking if they needed a drummer, but I never actually mailed any. I figured if things were to happen they would just fall into place. But how the heck was any band to know that I wanted to be in the scene again and play drums. I eventually was asked to stop writing reviews for Punk Planet in the early 00's as my last few were a few lines (at times including how I felt about anything from food to what clothes the bands wore in their promo shot). Yeah I was really burnt out. I pointed out that even if I loved the CD or record it might sell two or three more copies so who gave a shit? That is something even the indie label reps didn't want to read. I can tell you after spending time in the studio working on your music and paying postage to send it into a magazine hoping to finally see your name in print it must have sucked to then open up the following months issue only to find the reviewer talking about Andre the Giant and burritos in your review. This critic knew he was wrong.

"It's all about the rock game" -Oblivion

"I know this guy who lives across the street who plays guitar."

I was hanging out spring of 1988 at a high school friend's house named Bob (the guy not the house). It was well known around in several of my nerd and jock circles that I was looking to play in a band. Sure I was in concert and marching bands in high school, but I really wanted to be in a real live rock band. You know, a group of youngsters that play music that old people hate. When's the last time you heard some old lady church group protest a marching band?

I wanted so badly to join a band so that I could meet girls, get rich, and change then world— and it didn't even have to be in that order.

Up until then I had tried to form a high school band "Avalon" (band names are so fun to come up with) with a bunch of friends who didn't play any instruments or were in the process of just learning. It never took off more than me writing the name Avalon on my gym shoes. I made it look all badass with flowing lettering. And of course I had spent hours upon hours of my youth up until and including this time, pretending to be in a band. I would hit pillows with drumsticks or if my family wasn't around, I would try to play my actual drum set. It sat in the corner of the basement. A sparkly blue 4 piece Whitehall drum set that I had bought for 100 bucks with money from doing a paper routs and working as a locker room boy at the local community pool. Community pools are disgusting places filled with germs from baby fecal by the way.

For a while I had taken this large cardboard box and made it into a wall of sorts around my drum set. On this wall, I hung many rock and metal poster as I banged the hell out my kit and pretended to be in those bands. Pretending obviously as Rush, Iron Maiden, Bad Company, Helloween, and Led Zeppelin still haven't called me. Damn fools, they will all be dead soon, so they need to hurry!

So hearing that my friend here actually knew someone who could get real live rock and roll sounds from a guitar impressed me. I told him I would for sure be very interested in meeting this mysterious rock neighbor of his. He informed me that Scott went to St Joes (the evil twin, well actually the good Christian alternative to my very hellish public H.S, I went to, Proviso West.)

We eventually met and hit it off. Scott's shy and calm demeanor could jump instantly to a quirky dry but silly English type of humor. We hung out a few times and he eventually stopped over with his guitar and a small amp. It wasn't long before we came up with a short list of mostly Who and AC/DC tunes that we could jam to. After a practice or two in my basement, Scott asked me if I'd like to meet his friend Pete who was learning the bass. When I first met Pete there were several things that caught my attention. He is very smart, eccentric, and later how one friend would describe him as "big bird on acid," seemed to fit. It seems that they had a band they wanted to call Oblivion (but somehow I thought they were going to call it Alien's Picnic and wrote that on my gym shoes the following week in study hall.)

They had a drummer Tre (who would later actually play for a while in the Chicago punk band The Vindictives, but I am jumping way ahead in the story here.) So Tre wanted to spend some time practicing for a drum team and wouldn't have much time to practice for this girl's sweet 16 party, which is why the band Oblivion formed. Rock and roll is almost always about girls in some way.

Wow, not only could I join a band, but also we had a real gig on the horizon. Someone pinch me, and also help me write O B L I V I O N on my gym shoes.

We started off practicing as a band in Scott's garage and also in my basement, as long as we could before parents, neighbors, or police told us to stop. It was very repetitive playing the same songs over and over, but fun. It's a great feeling to play in a band for the first time. It is like a big "fuck you" to the normal world, and now the creative juices start flowing as now we can make our own music. And of course you get that feeling that you've become some kind of outlaw badass. Girls dig bad asses.

As a drummer it was cool to hit things and actually hear sounds somewhat similar to the ones you would hear coming from your record player. And add to that a guitar and some vocals and you got a band trying to recreate your favorite songs. You know that stupid but excited face kids have when they realize they are riding a bike for the first time after spending months or years on training wheels? Well, I am sure I had that face.

I did the dorky drummer thing where I would walk around high school with drumsticks in my back pocket hoping some cute girl would ask me if I was in a band. I only remember doing it a few times, but I also remember none of those times ever ended with a girl asking me if I was in a band. I do remember my friends slipping the sticks out of my tight blue jeans pocket and smacking the hell out of me with them.

The Who, Cheap Trick and AC/DC songs made up our early attempts at covering rock music. As we grew closer to the big gig we tossed in an Ace Frehley solo song as well as a Billy and the Boingers song (I know who the hell are Billy and...well, just google it). Pete was taking up most of the singing duties, and we weren't sure if we would add new members, but for the sweet 16 party gig on August 27, 1988, the line up would be Scott guitars/some vocals, Pete bass and main vocals, and myself as the drummer. We would be a power trio as they called it, but anyone listening to our skinny asses would question the whole power part at the moment.

Who would have thought back then, that staying a threesome would be the only way we ever did things. Well, besides the added keyboard at times which Pete would handle just like Rush's Geddy Lee but with a smaller nose and much lower voice.

I was hanging out with Pete a lot as the party drew near even when we didn't have practices. Scott was in a community church band so often after or before practices he would go from playing rock guitar to playing church sax. Pete and I would leave practice and go to Taco Bell or some record store and spend what little money we had. It was in Pete's room that I first saw an internet chat room and a cd player, technology now that seems real dated. I also noticed his wacked out sense of humor in how he would interact with his parents who seemed to be older that the average parents due to Pete being the baby like me in a way.

His brother Chris would talk about bands like Ministry and the Revolting Cocks, who would play a small role in transforming our sound in a few years.

Before we knew it, that August day popped up and we had our first gig. I drove my parents' van down Wolf Road knowing that this is what I wanted to do for the rest of my life. Drive my parents van down Wolf Road? No I wanted to rock!

I would take it gig by gig and thought that today we shall set the place on fire. Ok, so we played a living room and the crowd was a handful of her H.S. friends that went from standing in the living room for the show to often leaving the room to go grab cheese puffs from the kitchen, or more realistically escape our loud annoying sounds. Not many memories are left due to that being back in 1988, but I do recall having to play a drum solo (god help us all) and after it, looking down at their nice white carpet noticing a huge black stain I was leaving with my kick drum's foot peddle.

The thought of some of the more jockey or preppy kids not liking us only made me feel better as rock and roll isn't supposed to be for everyone, and it really wasn't for them. We were setting ourselves apart from the normal pack of kids. Take that you sweet sixteen partygoers!

After the show we packed up our gear and only a few of the kids felt obligated enough in some strange way to lie to us and tell us that we did great. We had some more practices, and even twice tried to add a fourth member to the band but it never felt right. Six months later, we got our first real club gig. Odyssey 1 under age night club (they spelled it N.I.T.E.) in Naperville, Illinois. It was known as a rich kid's version of a suburban metal bar. Perfect for us. The lineup was solid with us opening and bands called Aphasia, Dorian Grey and Cimax to follow. I always wondered if the band Cimax originally called themselves Climax and just dropped the "l" to stay more metal, as dropping letters but always having plenty of x's in your name was way metal back then.

I was all excited to play a stage as for sure shortly after this stage we would be loved and it would be stage after stage night after night. Well, that was as soon as I got out of high school. That first show saw us playing a lot of the same tunes with some added originals that we just learned the weeks before. We all were very nervous and forgetting the basics like breathing and smiling, but managed to get through the set alive.

Now, many times you will hear bands say that they can't describe their sound. That the music holds too many influences to really explain to the common listener. Usually it all means that they suck. Music styles are what they are and when people mess with them and mix it all up, they 99% of the time result in sounding really bad. Funk/Metal or Country/Rock anyone?

But I have to honestly say neither us, nor anyone who saw us, really knew what the heck we were playing in those early days. It would be three years later where a producer of a local music cable TV show would describe us as speed pop. Sounded fine with us.

It was a simple mix between basic rock and roll with some major and minor chords being explored along with this anything goes song structure. I am not saying our early music was great by any means, as we had a lot of growing to do and we choose to do it in front of what limited audiences were there to see the show at whatever club would have us. Smarter bands would have practiced a lot more in the basement or garage, coming up with some kind of sound before playing clubs, but we were too eager or at least I was to get the ball rolling. I had brought two girls to that show of which I had crushes on (stack up the odds ya' know) with one of them being my friend's little sister. But they had both gone the way of the crowd and gave us golf claps at best during our first show.

No one really liked us at all on that night or most of our early shows for that matter. But we seemed to know things will get better, and again did we really want a bunch of "we came to the glam rock party too late" type suburban metal heads to like us anyway? We would then play the local club Thirsty Whale (do whales even get thirsty?) The Thirsty Whale was a legendary metal club located in River Grove, IL on Grand Ave. More famous was Gene and Jude's, the hot dog stand next door, (which is still there.) The Whale is now a gas station, which one could now fill their tanks and buy a lottery card where glam metal gods such as Warrant and Poison once played. Heck, I even went to see Chicago's own major label- MTV glam effort

Enuff Z'nuff play there as well. Enuff Z'nuff was Chicago's answer to the mid to late 80's LA hair metal scene that boasted bands like Faster Pussycat, Motley Crue, and Ratt. They actually wrote some great rock songs behind their cheesy image and we liked the fact that even Chicago bands could get noticed on the national music scene. We always rooted for any of the local boys to break it big, which only a handful ever did. Since they broke out playing the Whale, we thought this might be the place for us. All throughout our career we took any shows we could get no matter what kind of bar or club or space they were in.

Another club that we held our early shows was called McGregor's, that club would be a major player in the punk scene at the time, but we were too ignorant to that kind of music at this point in our career, so we played with metal bands like Spellbound and Dutch Courage. We practiced some more and learned a few more classic rock covers and got a gig at yet another metal type club called Stay Out West in Hanover Park, Illinois. In their little back stage area we could see the same kind of cliques that we each experienced in high school. You had your cool kids (for this place it was the guys with the most hair spray and the girls with the best spandex pants) and you had your uncool losers like us. So the booker/owner of the place saw something entertaining in us and offered us another gig. We would play Stay Out West along with any other bar that would have us in those first few months, cutting our teeth as they say. Or pissing off the metal heads, as I would say. We didn't fit in, but we knew of nothing else. Unlike Pete and Scott who were a year older than me, I was still in High School in spring of 1989. I was the only kid in high School that played in a band that was actually getting club gigs. Most other bands were only playing parties or would rock out at the schools talent show or dumb shit like that. Sure our big club gig was something like a Tuesday night in front of 18 people at the Thirsty Whale, but it was a gig, and it felt like I was on my way.

We also made the mistake of accepting a Super Bowl show at Stay Out West. We thought, well there will be a ton of people there, so they would gladly want to see a young nobody band play. As the projector screen went up and we started our set, I could see the disappointed faces of the crowd saying put the screen back down so we could watch them funny commercials. We would end up playing behind the screen.

In August of 1989 we would go into the studio. Pete knew a guy who had a studio in his basement. This was before everyone and their mother could just record stuff on their computer and use various programs to mix it all down. Studios that a band like us could afford were very hard to find in the Chicago area. So off to record in Mt. Prospect we went for three Sundays in a row. The result would be our first demo tape. Also that summer, we took our first band photos. All the cool bands had a promo pack with their demo tapes as well as band photos they would post around town. We had a friend K.V. who had a camera and we all did various poses like sitting on a toilet trying to look cool and also posing in our underwear. No one said you had to look intelligent in your band photos. It would be many years before we would take any more band photos.

From those shows we met various other bands and would have to drag friends mostly from Pete's college (Pete and Scott were a year older than me as well as a year ahead of school, so they already knew college kids) to come and see us. The early days of any bands career puts a lot of strain on family and close friends. No one is coming early on because you are good, they mostly are doing it out of some strange moral obligation.

I was too shy to ask all my friends from school and work, of which I had limited numbers anyway. I did however, have a friend Glenn that I knew since grade school. He would come and video tape the shows with a huge ass video recorder. So early on, he was about it, as I certainly didn't want to be the guy who asked his parents to come to a show, as that is not rock and roll. Your parents are supposed to hate the music you like, and if you are in a band, they aren't supposed to like that either. If they dig it, it means your band is lame and you need to rock out a little more.

Speaking of parents, my dad passed away from cancer in November of 1989 as we were playing these lame shows. The normal world around me collapsed. I was devastated and felt like my whole childhood had ended and I was entering this adulthood thing without a father figure. He, coming from poverty, always taught me to be grateful for what you have, so I tried to be as grateful as I could for my 18 years with him. I was a freshman at the local junior college and Oblivion was a little over a year old. His passing threw me into a tailspin of depression and feeling all alone. Scott and Pete as well as the music we were making and listening to, were all there for me, and that is how I got through the tough times. Losing my dad put me into this sort of dazed feeling about my own future. I had just seen a man pass, who was working his ass off and was really waiting to have fun and adventures during his retirement which would have been just a few years down the line. From that I learned that if I ever had anything I wanted to do, I would just do it and not put it on any bucket list. Music was the only thing I liked and the only thing that made sense for me to do after losing him. His nine-to-five working class blues so to speak, wasn't going to be enough for me. I wanted to do something different, something I could enjoy every day. Never the less, had he lived longer, I still wouldn't have asked him to come to any of the shows as again having your parents there is lame!

Through my depression I somehow managed to carry on with my freshman year at Junior College, working the night shift at UPS, and of course playing my drums in Oblivion. I somehow managed to play a show just a week after my dad died. Music is always the best healer. It would have to be as I was in for a tough ride. That November 1989 show at the Thirsty Whale was also when this metal of all metal bands, Nitro, came back around unexpected and jumped on the bill as headliners. This night would go from something we used to impress metal heads to get other shows, to a soon turned into a joke for the punk crowd, when we could say that Oblivion opened for Nitro. For those of you out of the loop, go to YouTube and search Nitro-Freight Train, and then thank me later after you stop laughing.

We worked hard at getting more shows and trying to get our name out there. We were still kind of shy about the band and knew we had a long way to go. We would promote the band within our circle of friends and not too much outside of that. I spent that Christmas in 1989 with Pete driving me to the Alley store in Chicago (when it was only a small place in a so-so neighborhood and not the city alternative like shopping mall it is now.) We placed some flyers for our next show amongst all the other literature and ads in the doorway. We would soon learn that it takes a lot more than putting a flyer somewhere to get people to check out your band. It's always an interesting moment when you realize some strangers are showing up to your show either because they somehow like your music or they heard it as a good time. If you think about it, only a handful of all the bands that get created even make it to a stage in some bar. Then even a smaller percentage of them actually get people who they aren't related to, or sleeping with, to show up and listen to their music. And of course the lucky ones get many people to be able to show up night after night all around this crazy world. It took Oblivion two to three years to start to get this. This is when I thought we just might have a chance of breaking out of the suburban nightmare of playing alongside bad metal and cover bands if we could only get these few people to tell some others we could ask the 10-20 people to follow us into the city where we were looking to finally play.

Our first demo tape finally came out in 1990. It was what you would expect from a band still growing and still in need of a lot of practicing. A lot of practicing. Six songs all over the rock spectrum filled with too much reverb and not enough balls. We immediately put together a promo package calling ourselves "A New and Original Sound of Hard Rock." What idiots we were.

We also couldn't wait to make another demo tape, so we could quickly move forward from our first one. We were still trying to play out as much as possible and landed a gig in the spring of 1990 at I.M.S.A. Illinois Mathematics and Science Academy. A place where all the students look like the singer from Weezer. I have the show on tape and I laugh every time I sit to watch a few minutes of it. Not from the sight of a young band's performance (which included this new and original style of hard rock along with some AC/DC, Cheap Trick, and Devo songs) and also not from the small moronic dancing pit of people in front of this large auditorium stage. I laugh because I remember playing the drums and hearing our roadie having the time of his life backstage just behind the curtain behind me, throwing around various stage props and laughing as he punched the stuffing out of some stuffed animals also left back there from some school play. We as a band would be known for the crazy people we seemed to conjure up. What we lacked early on in cheesy rock attributes like groupies and drug usage, we made up for by bringing to the party the most unusual characters you would ever find. We spent the spring and summer trying to get as many shows as we could. We usually got some opening slot on a weeknight, but we took what we could get and kept going, as we knew things would eventually change.

One night in late 1990 while driving home from my job at UPS, I heard this song on the radio from a local college station. It was awesome. Something like basic rock and roll, but it had a little more rawness and power to it. I just had to know what the hell it was. I pulled my car over and grabbed a pencil and wrote on the back of a candy wrapper the song name "Someday" from a local band called Sludgeworth. I know I spelled it all wrong, but I had the gist of it and the next day I was on my search for it. I had a friend that worked at a local store called Beyond the Limit and she told me they had this Sludgeworth record in stock. And not only that, but she also told me they were playing soon nearby in Elmhurst, Illinois at McGregor's. I listened to that 7- inch nonstop for the next few weeks. All I could compare it to in my new young limited punk and alternative mind was to the Plimsouls song "A Million Miles Away" that I heard in the movie *Valley Girl*. The sounds coming from my stereo was rock, but not as polished and cleaned up as the stuff I was listening to on the radio. To me it seemed more real and honest. I had known about punk rock in a general way. I heard about the Sex Pistols and even owned a Sid Viscous shirt I wore when I wanted to show everyone how different I was. I was a huge fan of the movie *Sid and Nancy* and thought The Sex Pistols had the perfect attitude and image for rock. I knew the basic hits catalog from bands like The Clash and The Ramones, but I had no idea that the Chicago area had a punk scene as well. I was not aware that punk rock had survived the 80's and was still going strong in the underground. I was hoping that Oblivion, meaning Pete, might want to try writing a song or two with that same kind of raw feel. Pete and I were also listening to this obscure punk band called Shamrock Shakes. They had a pop punk style filled with goofy lyrics. Their sound was again, something I was not hearing on the major radio stations. Pete and I both made plans to see this Sludgeworth band on December 30th. Another band, The Gore Gore Girls who had this Ben Weasel guy in it, would play along with Screeching Weasel that night. It was a packed show and the people got into these opening bands and then Sludgeworth came out. The jammed in crowd pushed us all around and I was a little afraid of this new scene and activities they did, but not too much to take away from the newness and excitement of it all. The kids seem to be harmless as long as you didn't get smashed into the railings that surrounded the small stage. The response given to the band was exactly what we wanted for Oblivion. To play in front of excited people who seemed to give a shit about your

95

band and music. We were on a mission. After the show, we felt like we just had a life changing experience. On the way to Pete's car this guy (who I would later find out to be Martin from Los Crudos) asked me if I wanted to buy a record. I was broke but so blown away by the sounds I had just heard that I used my Taco Bell money (anytime I hung out with Pete and he drove, the night always included a stop at the bell) to buy this local comp 7-inch called *There's a Fungus Among Us*. I brought it home and played that along with my Sludgeworth record over and over and over. Pete's brother had a friend who lent me a Naked Raygun record and my education in Chicago punk was starting. We made plans to come back to see more punk shows at McGregor's. The scene of sweaty hyper kids pushing into each other and yelling the lyrics to the songs right back at the band was impressive given the fact that we were playing places that loud clapping and an occasional "You guys Rock" (never aimed at us mind you) was about as crazy as it got. I even got to see some boobies at McGregor's, when Screeching Weasel played this song "I Wanna Be Naked" some pretty blond girl in the back (who I would later found out to be their next drummer's sister) lifted up her shirt to show of her goods. Wow! Boobs and fast energetic music, I really found my scene! An important note, those boobs would be the only ones I have ever seen flashed, as in my 10+ years with Oblivion, the only boobs flashed were man boobs in the pit. Oh well.

So again, in the parking lot we were handed flyers and asked if we would come back to see this band everyone was talking about called Pegboy. They were a new super group of sorts with members from other past punk bands Naked Raygun and Bhopal Stiffs. I bought their *Three Card Monte EP*, and it joined the other punk records nonstop playing on my turntable. The punchy wall of power guitar sound from John Haggerty was what I thought would be perfect for Oblivion. At the time our guitar sound was dependent on how Scott's amp head was set. Since we were still learning our craft, and it for me was often too distorted, I would try to turn the nobs when no one was around after practice ever so slightly to what I thought would be a better sound. But it seemed Scott always knew where he left them and would change them back. How did he know?

The pressure of getting shows and advancing our sound was at times getting to us. One night Scott left a note on his amp letting Pete and I know that he was thinking of leaving the band, as maybe we should find another guitar player. We never even mentioned it as like it or not it, it was going to be us three until the end.

I loved the sense of community I felt at these shows. I wasn't making friends that much, but I still felt connected to the other people in the crowd here and also even at bigger venues like the Metro and Riv that Raygun would play at.

I still stood out a little. Never feeling the need though to dress the part of the punks at the shows in their blue jeans, leather jacket and black t-shirt of their favorite punk band, I proudly wore my Willie Nelson and Culture Club t-shirts along with whatever dumb ass looking out of style shorts my mom had picked up for me at the flea market.

Oblivion called McGregor's trying to get on a punk show, and I guess with our metal sounding name they passed along to this promoter named Joey. He put us on a non-punk show with some lame metal bands and we had a bad time. We were close, but still so far away. To try to stay on the promoter's good side, we agreed to do this pay to play sort of bullshit where we would sell tickets to our "fans" in exchange for playing this place called the Gateway Theatre in Chicago. We wanted a city gig as well as wanted to impress this booker so he might finally put us on a punk night. Our first official city gig was at this small bar near the Vic Theatre called "Union." We had seen our alternative metal buddies I Speak Jive play there and thought it would be cool. It was cool, because they had friends and a crowd, we really had neither, but there was something about playing the big city. We knew that was where we needed to keep playing. We knew the city clubs were a better fit for the direction for the band. City folk seemed a little more interested in original music while out in the burbs they would be happy to hear Journey and Boston covers all night, and I think they still prefer it that way.

Speaking of original music, our second demo *Neighborhood* finally came out in July 1991, and it showed more promise than the first one. The production was a little better as we were slowly learning how to ask for the sound we wanted.

Four songs (including I'll Be Waiting for You" which we would re-record on our next tape) from a band that was in a transitional period given our different surroundings. We were still playing lame shows but we were now attending some excellent ones. The scene around us was also evolving and exploding. Chicago bands like Smashing Pumpkins and Material Issue were growing and gaining national exposure to the Chicago music scene. Both bands had released their debut full length CD's and both were excellent. Any attention to a scene brings both bad and good, and we were hoping to let the good of it all help our cause of gaining more fans.

As for the punk scene, Screeching Weasel was back with what is one of the best records ever made in any genre with My Brain Hurts. In your face melodic sing along punk rock. A perfect record that joined my collection near my turntable.

In my own little personal world, I was also evolving.

I was head over heels over this girl Fay I recently met who was a Canadian exchange student at Pete's college. It was love, or really intense liking at first sight. At 20, who really knows what love is anyway. So if I wasn't at school, work, or doing band stuff I was with her. Not sure how much being in a band helped me look interesting to others, but I did notice a guy like me with limited looks could seem to be interesting enough to date by girls with a much better appearance than myself. I was still hanging out with Pete at shows and going record shopping when my budget allowed.

We ventured out to see Screeching Weasel and Sludgeworth share the bill at on over 21 show in 1991. I used the old speeding ticket change the birthday date thingy to make myself a year older so I could get in. There were maybe 8 people there with Pete and myself glued to the front of the area that would be considered the stage. We learned that this energetic punk stuff wasn't really pulling in the over 21 crowd who wanted to sit there and have a beer over talking politics. Some bands could draw the older guys (older meaning like 22 to 35) like Raygun, but most found their crowd to be of the younger sort. They ate this speedy pop punk stuff up like a fat kid sitting in front of a plate of Twinkies.

Our sound wasn't really going to be straight ahead punk rock, as we had too many musical influences that we were trying to pull off) but we knew the audience we wanted. The crazy kids.

So we sold just a few tickets to this Gateway show and later gave most of them away outside the show. We went on late and had our skate boarding friend "Marfa" bring a dummy on stage and stage dive with it. I still have video footage of this show and musically it sucked, but atmosphere we were finally becoming a band that would entertain the freaks. After realizing we didn't want to become anyone's little bitch band by paying to play, so we stopped playing these types of places with those kind of L.A. want to be promoters and never looked back.

As you have by now read, I joined the Bollweevils in October of 1991, so that helped introduce me to the D.I.Y. (Do It Yourself) ethic of the punk scene where Oblivion was heading. I should also mention for point of reference in the bigger picture that Nirvana's "Smells Like Teen Spirit" was taking MTV and the nation by storm. The trickle-down effect would soon hit the local scene in that the kids that followed trends would soon be on the lookout for alternative and punk bands playing around town, so they could be cool. The national and local underground scene was about to get a little light on it and grow some. For Oblivion, 1991 ended with a December show at the Thirsty Whale that was actually good as we found some cool metal bands to play with and the crowd was slowly noticing something different, but oddly entertaining about us. Playing in front of a crowd was not embarrassing me.

We even tried to get some of the few bands we liked and met in the metal scene to come with us into this new world, not really caring if the punk crowd gave them a chance or not, but that never worked out so well. One band came along as I Speak Jive played with us and The Vindictives once. The punkers waiting for The Vindictives straight ahead punk rock attack didn't like I Speak Jive's more alternative metal approach to music. I Speak Jive was one of the few bands that could pull off the metal/alternative thing. They were led by one of those crazy type singers in this guy J.R. He loved to push buttons. They had this song in which somehow the lyrics called for J.R. to make out with someone that was supposed to be his brother. Now mind you this was the early 90's so the music and entertainment world was still a little conservative towards anything considered gay. Especially the macho world of most punk shows.

So J.R. and I Speak Jive had taken our advice and ventured out to play some of the same clubs we were and at Off The Alley they performed in front of a mostly punk crowd who like at The Vindictives show, was not getting into these metal head freaks. Before the show I noticed the usual brother guy wasn't there and I told J.R. if he needed a fill in I was game for the sake of art but no open mouth, just a peck and get on with it. So of course the end of the set comes and the song kicks in and good ole J.R. comes over to me standing at the side of the stage and he plants one on me and then squeezes my cheeks forcing my mouth open. "Oh shit," I thought, So much for no open mouth.

After my first and only man kiss (not that there's anything wrong with it) I jumped off the stage and onto the top of the packed crowd. Some of the skin head types in the pit were trying to pull me towards them and I could hear some calling me fag, so the crowd that was actually digging the show in the front rows forced me up on back onto the stage before the hairless pit monsters could get to me. It was one of my few but probably my best crowd surfing moment.

It is funny looking back now as I would venture no one would care anymore about most of these things. The scene has opened up a lot for the most part. Our next shows were in basements or garages. We were full into the punk scene now. I loved everything about it. The dirty smell, the semi dangerous feel it still had at that time, and the whole newness to it all.

1992 had me going into Attica studio with both bands to record. Through the Weevils I met Chuck, a guitar player in a punk band no Empathy who also recorded bands out of an Attic in the Wicker Park area of Chicago. Oblivion wanted a more meat and potatoes punk sound and less of a band trying to fit into the suburban metal scene. Chuck and this upstairs room was the perfect fit for our next demo. I just wish hauling all my drums up from my car on the street to this third floor attic was easier. I also turned 21 in March of 1992 and could finally now legally go out to various dance clubs in the city. Pete and I danced (or moved around like idiots) at Exit (old location), NEO, and this place called 950. We didn't like a lot of the alternative or goth songs played, but when they cued up Pegboy's "Through My Fingers, or REVCO's "Beers Steers and Queers," usually in the last hour of the place being opened, you couldn't get us off the dance floor. We thought we were the outcast badass type, but just probably looked like two spastic nerds out on the dance floor. We would go from the closed club out to eat mostly at McDan's where they did an excellent breakfast for us clubbers and the hookers. Those were the days back in 90-93. Leather jackets and bad lipstick all served over some fried eggs. I would get home between three and four am and sleep a few hours before waking up for college classes that I didn't want to be at. I then would go to my UPS job from five to ten pm, which I would count the hours to the clock stuck 10 so I could race out to do it all over again.

I had this thing where I would speed on the 290 expressway so I could let my car coast and that way I could take my foot off the gas pedal and change out of work shorts and into my club clothes. Which usually consisted of blue jeans and some silly t-shirt. I got really good at changing clothes in the car. This was a skill I would use all the time when we started to play later shows. Going from work to a gig. When I started wearing fake leather pants for a short while, that sucked, as putting those things on were close to impossible let alone in car going over 80mph so I could glide for a while. Only once did I have to change from show to show. Bollweevils had a gig in Elgin once while Oblivion had a show 40 minutes away in Villa Park. I told myself to never allow two different shows at different places on the same night. It was a little too much like work.

I always tried my best to treat the bands as separate entities. It made sense for a booker to call me and try to get both bands to play the same show as it made their job easier to fill the three or four slots there were looking for. Especially when both bands started to draw their own crowds. I also didn't want the Bollweevil guys to think the only reason I joined the band was to promote Oblivion.

As for me and Pete "dancing" our dance moves included the slam dance or pogo where it was not only popular at these alternative clubs but also at concerts. Pits and jumping off of whatever kind of stage was provided was soon becoming the thing to do at these early 90's punk shows. Soon it would become the norm as well as you would see it in TV ads, but for now it was a thing of the underground scene in the metal and punk communities. I went to a show at the Riv back in late 1990, which featured the Dead Milkmen and Mojo Nixon. I remember Mojo Nixon was taken aback by the pit and crowd surfers and asked the crowd if he could do it. He jumped in and floated around during a guitar solo break and it brought the unity of a performer and an audience together. It was cool back then. The local clubs were also taking advantage of the explosion of the alternative bands as they were overselling shows to get a few extra bucks. Jesus Jones (yeah I went to see them) and Green Day at the Vic in the early 90's bring back memories of just getting enough air into my lungs so that I could breathe. The smell of sweat and pot filled those clubs, and often the stench would stay in your clothes even after washing them.

The pit was always the place to be even if you had to pay a price. Naked Raygun shows always had a wall of death, which would be mostly fat guys with really short hair also known as skinheads. They would back up about 20 feet or so and just run forward like a herd of pissed off cows and smoosh us skinny kids in the front into the barricades during the first song. The worse was when I went with Billy Blastoff to see Murphy's Law play the Vic in January 1992. It was like a controlled crowd riot with people jumping from anything that wasn't tied down. Idiots landing on your head from all angles forcing your neck to jerk to one side. It was something, a painful something.

In the spring of 1992, I had to say goodbye to my on and off girlfriend as she graduated college went back home to Toronto. My heart was broke, but a broken heart or two does a musician good. Music was back to being my full time girlfriend and the love of my life. I tried to go out as often as I could to help get me out of the dumps. I wondered why life just couldn't be simple? Find someone, love them, spend your life happy in the suburbs and have a nice house and a dumb dog that fetches sticks. Friends told me to snap out of it as they liked me better without a girlfriend anyway, as I seemed to go out and party a lot more as a single lad. I was losing interest in school as I thought nothing I am learning in college is as fun as playing a good show. Maybe this music thing could very well turn into a career? Playing shows was sure a lot more fun than trying to stay awake during lectures. And also there didn't seem to be a lot of careers where people clapped and shouted for you as you did your job.

Being on a stage was also helping me overcome my shyness. People introduced me at college parties as Pete's drummer, the drummer from Oblivion or drummer from Bollweevils. I was finally somebody. Rock music had given me personality. I could act however I wanted. People expect band guys to be a little nuts. People want band guys to be a little nuts. They want you to be the guy at the party who puts on a pink G-string over your fake leather pants you bought at the sexy clothes shop next to The Alley store which also had a neat o little pocket in the front that chips were placed in and then party goes ate the chips out of the G-string as I stumbled around. They really do want you to be that guy, so I was happy to oblige to be goofy both on a stage and off. And often I had my band mates Pete and Scott next to me in my pursuit of silliness. Oblivion was also now not afraid to be the same jackasses we were off stage, onstage. We relaxed and brought that same banter we had with our friends in my basement shows to the crowd at our club shows. I was able to have basement shows as I was paying my mom like 50 bucks rent to still be able to live at home while I went to college. She was only home at this point six months out of the year as she now had a small condo in Florida, which is something I think by law all old people have to have.

So I planned all these basement shows and parties at times in which I would have weeks, even months to clean up the house before mom came back. All my worlds were colliding, as people I knew from both bands were now all mingling among other things in my basement. As one band would end practice the other would show up. At times we had these odd jam sessions in the middle with members from both bands as well as some other friends. I met a girl Alecia, who I would go out clubbing with on occasion, through one of my artist friends John. Alecia would also take some photos of the band that would end up as the insert for our future "*Product*" 7- inch. Her brother Dan was the guitar player for 88 Fingers Louie who I already knew of the 88 Fingers crew from the Bollweevil gang as well as previously mentioned, I hosted their first gig at my basement. It seemed the scene was all connected and somehow Oblivion and our non punk asses got into it.

When we weren't in the basement I noticed kids at the punk shows were talking about this new band Oblivion and it seemed if they liked us musically or not they mostly agreed we were a band to check out live. While I didn't feel like a new band so to speak, I was glad the punks were taking notice.

Our third and final demo tape came out *Think Tightrope Boobjob*. That title was something. We all came up with one word and blended it in. Many people thought my word was "boobjob'" since I was always making sexual jokes and generally being a little pervert. But my word was Think. I kind of was into those one-word titles like Breathe from Ministry and most of the Jesus Lizard catalog.

Pete came up with Tightrope and Scott with Boobjob.

I believe Pete drew the tape's cover as well. Five songs that we were actually very proud of.

I was proud enough of it that I dubbed some copies to hand out at the big touring Lollapalooza festival which was in its second year. What a brilliant plan I had. With the Seattle scene bands like Pearl Jam and Soundgarden sharing the main stage with Chicago industrial heroes Ministry, I thought the mixed crowd would love our sound. Becoming popular and hitting it in the music industry seemed so simple to me. Here you had this festival bringing together all the fans we would ever want all in one place. All the hard work in gathering everyone was already done. All I had to do was supply them alternative masses with the music I know they would all want to hear. I made 20 copies and handed them out in the parking lot before the show. I hoped if anyone really liked it they would make copies for their friends, as nothing sounds better than a cassette copy of a copy of a copy. Years later someone would actually come up to me and say that they were one of the twenty kids that got a tape that day. See, I knew it was worth it.

Even with my massive tape hand out, the local shows were still small. Our loyal friends were getting burnt out I think, so we needed to make some new fans soon. We set up a show at the basement of Pete's college with The Vindictives in October so that these kids would simply have to come down from their dorm rooms to check it out and not worry about driving to some lame bar to see us. We knew we had to start doing things differently to gather some attention. We needed to record a record, as all the cool punk bands had vinyl out. We started working on the songs.

Along with band life, true to form I found another girlfriend. This one wasn't an exchange student but rather someone who had been a friend for a while and if I wasn't at school or work I was in her dorm room back at Pete's college. For someone who never went away to college, I did spend a lot of my time hanging out in those tiny dorm rooms at Rosary College. Once someone in a food line asked me when I was going to graduate, and I had to tell him, "Dude, I don't even go here."

It was in Nicole's room where I would listen to Green Day's *Kerplunk* tape over and over, glad that the punk scene seemed to love this band. I thought they were a simple pop rock band, and if the kids accepted them, then maybe Oblivion's speedy rock/pop sound wouldn't come off as too wimpy then.

I was finding it hard to make time for every aspect of my life. Two bands, one job, one college, a girlfriend, and a single dream of somehow making it in music.

But all good things come to an end and as 1992 ended, so did my relationship with Nicole. Cue up the sad songs and bring on another heartbreak please.

My friends were glad to have the nutty single Brian back and I was counting on music once again to help with the hurt. I think it's easier to date non-friends if that makes sense, as when this relationship ended with such a great friend, it sucked. I wanted to use these emotions of depression of a love lost for my own benefit. I tried writing songs for the band and soon discovered I sucked at lyrics. Unless you find something deep in the following. "Like Christopher Robin to his friend Pooh, All I want to do is be the honey for you."

No wonder she dumped me, who the fuck writes lyrics about Pooh?

1993 started off with me back at McGregor's watching what was billed as Sludgeworth's last show. I couldn't believe my favorite local punk band was calling it quits. They had just sent me a Christmas card, this couldn't be!

I was also finally out of junior college with my big bad associate of liberal arts degree and now sleeping, I mean attending lectures at U.I.C. in Chicago. Even though I didn't think I would need one, I was working towards a journalism degree to fall back on, but I knew this drumming thing would come through eventually. It had to.

Oblivion entered Attica studios with Chuck recording us again and on two Sundays in a row in January we recorded and mixed what would be our first 7-inch record. Three songs we all felt rocked and for the first time I actually liked everything about our release, as it was a vinyl record along with some cool art and photos. The cover featured all of us in new stories and mine was actually a takeoff on an actual Chicago Sun Times article that was done about me a month before.

It was goodbye and good riddance to the demo tape days. Through playing some local shows with No Empathy (a band that Chuck, our producer, played guitar in.) Pete had struck up multiple conversations with their singer Marc Ruvolo who operated Johann's Face Records along with his friend Gar.

Since Sludgeworth had called it quits the label was looking for other bands to promote. We were more than willing to try to make something to sell to the kids. Which is why we called our first 7-inch *Product,* as low key and humble the punk community was, we wanted to make no excuses. We made this little three-song record for people to buy. We had just entered the world of consumption. Our *"Product"* would be out there with all the other crap to buy like other bands records, CD's, shirts, etc.

I remember bringing home the test pressing and just holding it like a proud parent would hold its newborn, for a long time before putting it onto my old turntable. I always thought vinyl was the big time, even after CD's came out. Johann's Face would help distribute and sell the 7-inch and they would put it in their catalog which at the time was getting some attention due to the *Ben Weasel Don't Like It* 7- inch by Marc's band No Empathy. Marc was in a lot of bands. One being the strange sounding Chia Pet, which Scott would play in for some time as well as being in Oblivion.

I think we would split the profits on our 7- inch 50/50 (like there ever was any) after all cost were settled. But since we always paid for the studio ourselves, it was usually the deal where we got half the pressings to sell on our own.

Shows started picking up and we were gaining fans pretty much every time we played. The punk kids liked the faster songs we were playing at the time like "She's Moving to Paris" from our last tape and "Theodore" off of our new *Product*. The song "Fester" with its funky ending refrain of "Gotta new pair of shoes...gotta new pair of shoes" became a little sing along. I was also glad it never became too much of an audience participation number in that I had to duck only a few times from flying shoes coming at me. The scene was quick to call sell out if you were playing anything too mainstream. Even though funky rhythmic alternative sounds like the Red Hot Chili Peppers and Jane's Addiction were breaking it big around then, we always seemed to get away with making any kind of rhythm or style seem ok for the most part to our little growing punk crowd. They always seemed to know we weren't playing some flavor of the month style just to gain some kind of popularity. The 7-inch for the most part did what we wanted it to do which was to simply add our name to the local scene. Around this time was also when word spread about our energetic live show and also Pete's wacky personality. To me, I don't know how bands could not want to be energetic and fun, but so many bands back then were taking themselves too seriously, so it was easy to separate yourself from the pack.

I was also hearing people say that they liked the Weevils shows as well. Two for two, I was lucky not to be in any of those boring ass emo bands at the time.

"Our next song um.. This is a song about um. "

I hated that shit. Entertain me motherfuckers. I paid five bucks, now jump monkey boys, JUMP!

The early 1990's scene didn't have a lot of places willing to put on all age shows, even though the kind of music we all were playing was slowly becoming more accepted. There was still a fear of the punk scene and the trouble that it brought. McGregor's, the one suburban club willing to put on shows was closing, and most city places were 21 and over places which never really attracted the younger punk kids. The punk kids were noticing me now if I went to a record show or to see other bands play. I was the Bollweevil or Oblivion guy. I even would sign autographs when asked, and that always no lie, felt cool. Kids would ask when my next show was and if any records were coming out? It was fun for a social misfit to have a group of people like me and be interested in what I was doing. It never went to my head as all it took was to go to work or school where no one gave a shit, and one lonely walk down a hallway or warehouse would force me right back to normal life.

With the closing of one club and the scene growing there were mixed feelings about where bands should play. One night at a punk meeting (yup, they actually took place) people discussed options. So here are various members of bands all sitting around the Underdog Record's loft in Wicker Park throwing out rules and regulations. Ben Weasel and Joey Vindictive were set against telling the larger club The Metro to fuck off, if and when they asked any of the punk bands to help fill their venue. They had stories of the club's security beating up on the punk kids as well as something about them hating punks in an article in the local paper. Most of the people were on board and to be honest most of their bands would never be asked anyway. They both came over to me as I was in not only one, but two bands that were growing and gaining fans and would have the opportunity to play places like the Metro. As much as I admired them both, I told them that I could only really speak for Oblivion, and that we would be up for playing almost anywhere. And that it would seem hypocritical for us not to play a place that we would go to see other bands play at. I had seen Helmet, Buffalo Tom, Naked Raygun, Poster Children and countless other bands at the Metro. Besides the fact that we had friends who worked there, and from my past experiences some of the punk kids were assholes at shows so who knows who was right and wrong in every instance.

We had already sent The Metro booker a few of our tapes and were always getting these form rejection letters, but it was one of our goals to play there. Something about that stage there. We would finally get our first Metro gig later that year in October. It wasn't a big bad punk show but rather a friend of Pete's asked us to join the bill on some poorly attended Wednesday night. It was cool finally seeing what the backstage area looked like. It was for me like exploring Narnia or something. The small rooms weren't cool, but walking up the staircase that led to the stage was always exhilarating. Years later when my fiancée asked me why I was still doing it when the band seemed to be leveling out, I brought her onto that iconic Metro stage right before we walked out. To hear the excited people clapping and screaming, I think she got it as I looked at her wide grin. It for sure was a drug. A drug I was willing to do almost anything for.

Our next 7-inch came out, 1993's *Full Blown Grover*. Only Pete's brain knows why that title stuck but when he told us the idea, no one had any better ideas. We all grew up on Sesame Street and loved that as well as the Muppets. Our generation was probably the first group of kids who parents would place them in front of the TV to act as the baby sitter. Pete would also make these mix tapes of various songs and banter between characters like Bert and Ernie. Strange parts of metal songs blended in with scenes from shows like Mr. Rogers. Some of the funniest shit ever. Again, only his head knew why or how to make these. They were a hit amongst our little messed up circle of college friends and we would listen to them over and over in their dorms.

Grover was a one-day recording affair on May 15th. This was the only time we brought our producer/engineer Chuck to a different place, as we recorded this one at Flat Iron Studios also in Chicago. I was getting used to playing drums in a studio. It was also calming to have Chuck record us, as by now we all saw him as the fourth member of the band so to speak. I never used a click track to record and I had this thing where I felt my best takes would be the second or third one. I always messed up something in the first take, but I did have some songs in later recordings that were first takes. I never liked staying too long in a studio, as I wanted the process to go fast so I could see the end result sooner.

We wanted the recordings to sound live and raw, but sometimes when you completely miss hitting a drum you just have to go back and do it again. As good as the other two slower tunes were, the only track that got attention was the first song "Fear of China."

We were all so excited to get another 7-inch out as well as finally put out that wacky "Fear of China" song to vinyl. People gravitated to it when we played it live and since it had both fast parts and silly slow parts, we knew we weren't painting ourselves into a corner with a certain sound.

My musical life was satisfying. My personal life well...I was still hanging out in my free time with many people who knew my x-girlfriend, so I had to play the game of try to avoid her in the college hallways. Every glimpse of her skinny frame and blond hair, sitting and chatting with our friends would set me back into wondering why things ended. For a 21-year-old boy, I sure was a little 15-year-old girl about relationships. I had a lot of other things to take my mind off of it all as both bands were playing and practicing weekly and I was going to every punk show I could find time to attend. I loved being so involved in the scene. I also had pretty much stopped buying any music from a major label artist, and was only giving my limited money to bands on smaller independent labels, or local bands. I felt like we would all overtake the corporate music world soon and show them that (to quote Killing Joke here) "Money is not our god."

In those early days we still had some slower songs and even songs with keyboards. So when we started to really find our sound, these newer songs didn't fit well with our older moody material. Our show was changing. We had also always loved doing covers, but did not want to become another suburban joke cover band. We wanted to really play our own music. We soon started to reduce the covers to like one to two a set and play around eight to ten originals. It takes a lot for a bands original songs to push through. People want to hear songs that they are familiar with. But if you want to be a band you have to make that jump sometime. Since we didn't always want to play the same set nor same songs we would still pull out some of our old (mind you, one to two years old) songs to fill in the gaps. I remember very well playing songs like "Don't Sit Down" (from *Full Blown Grover*) and "Censorship" (from our *Think...* demo tape) for the last time at a church basement show. It is funny how many punk shows were put on in either church basements or some kind of Christian youth Center.

We played with this local Western Suburb band called Herbal Flesh Tea who drew a small but diverse crowd. The punk kids that came to see us obviously liked some songs more than others. It sure is harder to make a slower song go over to a youthful and spastic crowd like that than a faster one.

We would miss playing those but Pete and Scott were writing new songs by the minute. Most songs we could work into becoming an Oblivion tune. We would record some practices and then listen back on how the songs came out. It was rare that we tossed any ideas away. Might have been a good thing for our friendships, but possible bad for the overall song choices. Still I feel we did way more good than bad and really that is all anyone can hope for when they put their craft out there for others to consume.

1993 was filled with shows of all kinds from church basements to kid's basements or garages, to small clubs that filled with 100 people to bigger ones with 1,000 people capacity. I was spending more time on stages than a stripper.

With all the fun I had on The Bollweevils tour that spring, I knew I had to plan for an Oblivion tour, I just didn't know how I would fit it all into my limited time off of work. Playing local shows was fun, but I was curious as to what out of state crowds would think of this Oblivion thing.

There's something about performing on a stage. Not that many punk bands get to do it as often shows are held in a basement, in a living room, in a garage etc...so real stages are few and far between. I always liked having some kind of platform to be on, even if it was one of the 6 inch wooden ones that always seem to bruise the shit out of the people's ankles in the front that got slammed into it.

I think it has to do with feeding the ego, and maybe so the people in the back can see, if you have enough people to come to the show to have "people in the back." I always giggle when I recall the great Andy Kaufman skit where he is the talk show host on this huge desk and the person being interviewed is several feet beneath him to let him know who is the star ya' know.

So anyways, you add a P.A. system to the whole stage thing and you get this sense of false power. I mean there is some power, as in front of the right crowd you could start a riot (I've seen it happen at some shows) if you wanted to, so there is some responsibility with it all. But it was always amusing and strange when people took you seriously just because you were up on a stage, or just because you are in a band. I loved it.

Speaking of stages, one of my favorite places to play was Wrigleyside in Chicago. Pete had a great idea to start a show series called "Calling All Creeps." It would feature three bands on Johann's Face Records. The Smoking Popes, No Empathy, and us, along with The Bollweevils opening the show up. It would be one of the few and final times both my bands played together. "Calling all Creeps 1" was such a success in June, that we soon booked another one for Halloween.

You couldn't fit another person in that small upstairs club. For me it was another success filled moment as I had just seen Sludeworth there a year before, and I hung outside in a long line down the block around the historic Wrigley Field with no one talking to me. I felt like someday I could be in a band that had people lined up outside, and by default someone would have to talk to me then. Plenty of people showed and plenty even talked to me at these classic "Calling All Creeps" shows. For many old time Oblivion fans the 1993 Halloween show was one of their all-time favorites with us playing in front of an crazed crowd as a guy dressed as Jesus played guitar behind us and another friend dressed as a priest ate a burrito on a trampoline. The stage divers also used the trampoline to launch themselves past the first few rows. That was until one kid slipped off of it mid jump and smashed his ribs on the stage monitors. Now that's entertainment!

Speaking of fucked up entertainment, I couldn't ever forget the show that took place just weeks before as Oblivion opened up for the openly gay band Pansy Division. It would start a friendship with the band that would last for years as we crossed paths touring a few times and always enjoyed hanging out and talking about metal music. I mention gay band as this band was loud and proud about it with their record covers, lyrics, and huge following in what was then called the Homocore punk scene. Even though all three of us (even Scott) were straight, we supported everyone's rights to have fun. The punk scene was at times a jock type mentality of boys pushing boys into each other and sometimes without knowing it turning the pit into a macho football like atmosphere that we all were trying to avoid. I believe we were the first band without any gay members to play a Homocore show. That night at the now closed Czar Bar on Division Street started off as any other with us unloading our gear and quickly looking for parking. The crowd quickly came in and we started our set. It was met with a nice reaction and we saw fitting that we pull out one of our older covers and end the night with our version of Y.M.C.A. I often played the drums with my head looking down after I summed up the crowd and made my glances around to look at people's faces to see their reaction to the band. As I lifted my head up during our final song all I saw was floppy penis, and then naked pale ass cheeks. This naked crowd surfer had placed himself on the now pogoing crowd filled with the local Gay community. So many eager people to grab his ass and pass him around above their cheering heads. His penis tossed from side to side as he rolled and made his way across the sea of uplifted hands. I couldn't help but smile and be more entertained by the happy go lucky crowd than by playing our cover song, as we finished our set.

Unfortunately the year ended on a down note. Joey Vindictive who had started his own club and record store in the city came up with a grand idea to have a $1.00 show with 18 bands featuring both my bands as well as Joey's band The Vindictives along with Lookout Record's (Green Day's former label) The Queers headlining. The Queers alone could have easily brought in the 300 to 400 kids needed to overfill that small venue. I arrived early as I was bringing some drum equipment as well as I was going to write about the event in hopes to get the national punk zine MRR to print it. Soon after it started at 2pm there were way too many kids in the club and over flowing onto the streets. A few hardcore bands played and the afternoon rolled on. As I was standing across the street waiting for some friends to show I see a cop car pull up and all kinds of other commotion. A kid had jumped out of a cab and not paid, so the cabbie called the cops to help track him down.

Kids were asking me if I saw the fight. I was confused. It seemed that Ben Weasel was hanging out with Joey in the store section. A local rapper who hung out in the punk crowd, Paul "Think", threw a pie at Ben's face. Ben and Joey caught up to him and words were exchanged and even punches thrown. And according to some stories a gun was involved. But the cop was there to find the kid to make him pay the cab fare. And of course this officer sees way too many funny looking people packed into a club with kids hanging out in the street and calls for backup. Back up comes and only after a few bands the show gets shut down, and I go home without playing to the masses and wonder if any zine would pick up a story about the whole mess. After talking to both Joey and Ben that week, I decided I couldn't get any story from the show, but soon after there were many versions in local zines of the pie throwing and police state that stopped the punks from having a good time.

1994 started off with my other activities getting me down. My university classes were finally getting to the point in which I had to study to keep up. Until now I was always one that could absorb enough information in class to be able to pass the class. But now my courses I needed to get my bachelor degree were too difficult. My Spanish speaking skills were minimal and I still don't know how I passed the first two semesters of it without being able to do nothing more than order a taco in Spanish. Maybe the teachers felt sorry for me. I also had to drop a class for the first time. I was in some strange Philosophy class where the instructor was all about having us read and assign math equations to different theories. My mind was mush. My scrawny body was also mush. I got in big trouble at UPS for causing some serious package damage when one night I was in a hurry to get to a show and basically threw every package that came down the conveyor belt to the same place on the steel grating and then down to the nearest belt out of my section. After they tracked down where all these damaged missorted boxes came from, I had some explaining to do. But since my reputation was good there, they all chalked it up to one bad night and I still had my part time job to pay my increasing bills. One of the bills was Oblivion going into the studio in January, but we always got a great rate on our studio time from Chuck. We were starting to record for what would be our first full-length record. Our big debut, and my first real chance at stardom as no one gets famous off of singles, you had to make a solid record both side A and B. (My how times have changed!)

Now, a lot of thought went into 7- inches, but a lot more would have to go into this record. We were honored to think that after selling some of our first two 7 inches that Johann's Face Records would be willing to put out a full record from us. Going from not being able to give away your first few cassette demos to having a local label wanting you to record a full length was a great feeling. It was starting to feel like this band thing just might work out, which was good because as previously mentioned school and work weren't going so great. We knew we would just come up with songs and not promise songs to anyone else for other projects until we had enough for a record, which for us meant 10 songs. Pete always liked how the band Jesus Lizard placed 10 songs on a record or cd. We wanted to go with 10 and also have an idea of playing them as side one and side two. In that we would order them to have a stronger song kick off and end both sides. And like our shows we wanted it to be quick and hopefully leave the listener with wanting to hear more.

"School" was one of the first things Pete came up with. Like "Fear of China" it had a slow section but was mostly a blazing speedy pop song which was soon becoming our signature sound

"School", for me represented the feeling of hanging out at Pete's college. My first few relationships were set with girls from there, as well as many of my weekend nights being single were spent hanging out in those hallways. I knew Scott and Pete would be able to come up with 10 songs on their own, but I gave it a shot in case for some odd reason this would be the only record we would ever make as I then would get my name in print. In Oblivion, no matter who wrote the songs we always kept it an even three way split as far as money was concerned.

Many times in bands the songwriters get the majority of the money or royalties from the music and the guys who just played their instruments on it got a much smaller share. I always appreciated Pete and Scott never taking this road with me, and really we never discussed it. It always seemed from the start that we knew writing songs or not we were all equally invested in this band. But nonetheless I tried to keep my end by churning out this song "Lost." In my abstract mind it could be a sort of Jesus Lizard meets Tool tune. I was also really into industrial Wax Trax Records sounds at the time. It came out much different but still entertaining. We had recorded the prophet Willie Townshend, a south side Chicago preacher off of his early morning radio show and in the studio the first time we placed it along with the music it just seemed to fit into its place. Which was good, as I never liked to spend more time that I had to editing things down. Who would have thought that the prophet would have long outlived the band, as I believe he is still yelling to people about the devil to this day.

We would do two days in the studio to kick things off and come back in a few months to finish it up. Attica studios had an artist living there and Marcus sorted through some photos and found one of what I think is his mom being scared by holding some parrots. The name Stop Thief came from Chuck hearing so many distinctive influences in our music that we decided to keep with the honest theme we had with calling our first 7- inch *Product. Stop Thief* was us admitting that all the newer music is just stolen parts from older music. We had no shame or trying to hide any pretentious acts on our part.

Speaking of pretentious, the Calling All Creep series Pete had started had been moved to the local big corporate club. Big for the scene meaning the Metro across from Chicago's landmark Wrigley Field, which held 1,100 plus happy go lucky kids. Mark from Johann's Face negotiated a five dollar cover charge with equal pay going to all the bands and no barricade in front of the stage. We took the lineup of Smoking Popes, No Empathy, us and with The Bollweevils doing very well with our own bigger shows we added Gauge to the opening slot. I also wrote to our emailing list (as I did with all our Metro shows) and told them if anyone felt like we were selling out and five bucks was too much, I could get them in for free. What I would do was have them come in around sound check time and leave the back door open for them which emptied into the alley besides the club. Only a few people ever took me up on this offer. The only thing we didn't like was the fact that the club tried to take a percentage of the money from items we sold such as cd's and t shirts, but we learned that if you give them a total and then bring in more, at the end of the night when they counted you could sometime make it seem that you only sold a couple of items. We knew all the tricks to keep the majority of what we saw as our money.

The record finally came out at the Wrigley Side Release show on July 3rd. Not sure if it had to do with Green Day and punk rock replacing Grunge rock as the flavor of choice for music in 1994, but the upstairs place was more packed with punk kids than ever. Later on the people who were at the bar on the first floor told stories of how the floor (their ceiling) was buckling to the people jumping up and down during our performance. Our set ended with the crowd rushing onto the small stage and signing the words to our final song that we never got to finish the song due to the people pulling out guitar chords and knocking over drums in their excited state. Soon after the club closed its doors to the punk shows and booked hippy guys with acoustic guitars that caused no damage to the buildings structure. As soon as one placed closed its doors to the scene, it seemed like another one quickly came up. And not just here in Chicago but in the whole tri-state area. And not only was I playing in shows in this new large area but my girlfriend search had also taken up a larger territory. I met this girl who would often come to various shows and she went to the University of Wisconsin. As I was hanging out in her room I noticed her looking at the clock a lot. I was feeling a connection happening as we did what all college age kids did, bullshit about life, politics, and how we just didn't get how the world could be so cruel to us all. I finally had to ask her what was up with all the clock checking and she said her sort of boyfriend might be coming over soon. I had my hoodie on and car keys out as she told me he usually comes over after football practice. The words 'guy" and "football" was all I needed to get the hell out of dodge. I just couldn't get any brakes in my personal life.

Oblivion finally lined up a tour with using some connections we found in the MRR magazine issue called "Book Your Own Fuckin' Life." It basically was a listing of people in towns all over the world that were willing to book you a punk show and or have you crash at their place. What a community this was. I had seen only a few local bands like 8-bark and some of the hard core bands tour. I learned it was possible for us smaller bands to do it. We asked Chuck to help come along and he actually said yes to our surprise. Chuck was a busy man recording local bands and playing in No Empathy along with helping national acts like Urge Overkill and Luscious Jackson.

We had mostly small shows and long drives set up along the East Coast and into the South East. None of the shows were as big as our hometown shows but we had a blast hanging out and playing night after night. Someone even halfheartedly tossed out the idea of touring more and possibly doing this full time. We all laughed at how fun it would be and somehow came up with a plan that if we could get another record out and still be having fun at this time next year, we would consider making the jump of quitting our jobs and going full time with the band. For me it seemed like a dream come true but I still had another long year to see it through.

We also came up with the idea of doing a Kiss tribute band, which I named KISSS. I wanted to keep it simple as most cover or tribute bands are named after a band's song, but I thought why not just call ourselves what the band calls themselves. I just added an extra "S" so that Gene Simmons wouldn't sue us. It happened after we played a show at a house party and the very drunk crowd wanted to hear between our sets so Chuck picked up Scott's guitar and me and Pete joined him in a few Kiss songs. Pete would be Gene, I was Peter, Chuck became Ace, and we somehow got local punk rocker Doug Ward (8-Bark) to somehow be Paul. But about that party...

Texas deserves its own part inside this Oblivion story since it played a major part in the band, as well as it's a big ass state. There is the rest of the US, and then there's Texas. Don't get me wrong Texas is great. A band could easily do a week or so on tour just in Texas alone. The state is too large for its own good. And for some reason there's always good tour stories that come out of that beer drinking, pickup truck driving state.

Oblivion usually for some strange reason went over very well in Texas. Texas is the home of Waco, a crazy town known for a horrible event between this whack job David Koresh and the US organization ATF.

Oblivion knew Waco as the town that had a big history with Dr. Pepper. The band's official drink, given they served it at Taco Bell. The band's official food. We took a tour of the Dr. Pepper museum once killing time between shows.

We loved it.

We loved Waco.

We loved Texas.

So mutual friends who were sisters and went to college with Pete came from Nacogdoches, Texas. The older sister was Maury who we honored in "Mauryland," even though when that song came out people thought we were talking about the dumb TV show host Maury Povich. We wanted to finally play a show in their hometown given all the support her and her sister had given us while being students near Chicago.

The show was a house party.

A Texas house party.

Two things stand out which to me sum up Texas. One being that before this party officially kicked in, many people showed up early to hang and start their drinking early and watch TV. On the tube was some interesting German fisting porn. It was a tape that the guy who hosted the party bought off of some dude that was trying to sell it at a local video shop, to no avail as the owner thought it was illegal here in the states. Trust me, after viewing it, it should have been if it wasn't. So there it was some "interesting" movie and by interesting I mean fucking disgusting, but still worth a gander to educate myself what was out there.

Nothing like finding yourself huddled in some house in Texas watching foreign adult movies with strangers. One of those moments.

Before playing as the people showed up there was this girl. I started talking her up and all, but when she found out I was the just drummer and that the singer was on the nearby couch, over she went to sweet talk Pete. Not that he and I ever had a competition, as we didn't always like the same kind of girls, but it was some sort of anti sex on the road thing we had in Oblivion. If one of us wasn't getting laid, it seemed none of us were getting laid. Sort of a punk rock cock block. So as I noticed this girl getting all into Pete, I mentioned to a friend that was there that it was shame such a pretty girl had herpes. He took me seriously and mentioned this to Pete when the girl was distracted. Pete made a b-line off of the couch.

I hated to throw a wrench in Pete's sleepy time rock star moves where he would fall asleep on the girl, but I had to amuse myself somehow in Texas. Not that my moves were any better. My move was to make them laugh, at any cost. Which seems harmless, but when you have a sick sense of humor that is seldom shared by the female species, you mostly just come across as a strange little fuck.

The night went on and the party was growing so large that people had to be ushered in at groups and then forced back out a few songs later. Our set soon became a covers set to keep the angry and happy drunks entertained. We noticed between sets, this drunk guy having a hard time standing as he was bleeding and holding his nose. His friend pulled him aside and as I stood outside looking over the crowd and waiting to play again, I overheard him tell his buddy that all he did was come out to another friend (a huge guy on the local football team), and he got punched. One might think that maybe a drunken party held in the south isn't the best place to decide to come out, but to each its own as I am not here to judge others, my dear readers, only to write about it.

So as this poor lad was telling his tale of how he got punched he was placing his hands on his friend's shoulder that also was becoming uneasy and started to push the guy away. Somehow from that I guess he got up the nerve to go back to this football friend and explain himself and not soon after his apologetic drunken tale came out of his mouth, that it was followed by another punch to the face. Not that someone getting punched in the face is funny, but what was funny is that person's reaction by yelling "What, what is it, why did you punch me" all while holding his swollen nose. "I told you to take your hands off of me...nobody care's" I guess no one cared that this guy was now coming out, but they did have a problem with being grabbed by a falling drunk.

As well as when drunk people tell you something it always comes with a lot of spit and repeating the same things over and over getting louder each time. Note to self: Give Texans room and no touching for god's sake.

Since I'm on Texas, we also had a show where we played the front porch of a trailer (big time, as if we were no bodies we would have played the back porch of a trailer). And this trailer was set in a horse ranch north of Dallas. Before the show I thought it was a good idea (being the animal lover I am) to go out and offer the horses some of my Triscuit crackers (back when they only had one flavor, the Triscuit flavor.)

I never had a group of horses run over to me so fast scaring the shit out of me. And like most intelligent animals they can sense your fear and give you a worse time because of it. Sort of an animal's way of messing with your dumb human ass. I was getting pushed and knocked around by these horses and thought one good kick would end me. At least I didn't punch them in the face for touching me I guess.

After the tour we had a taste for driving off and playing shows. A lot of our long time Chicago fans and friends had graduated and moved on with their lives, so it was time to make new juvenile friends and fans.

In October we had booked a show in London, Ontario and then Toronto and were doing them with our pals in Apocalypse Hoboken. The Hoboken boys became our favorite band to play with. We both had a love for the stupid things in life and their drunkenness entertained us a lot. Not to mention that their band kicked ass with a forceful dual guitar attack lead by the in your face vocal of their front man Todd Pott. They had a sense of humor mixed with a sense of danger about them.

Why they never made big time is just one of the many questions I have about great bands after all these years. We liked to play with bands that challenged us rather than go the route of asking bands that kind of sucked to open up for us. Some of the older fading bands we noticed did that so to still look good in front of their audience. The London show was fun but the barf pit in Toronto was a tad bit more memorable.

I spent the day driving up and then right before the gig I was hanging out with a former girlfriend (Fay, my former Canadian girlfriend, well she was still Canadian, just not my girlfriend anymore if you get it.) My stomach was already in knots, before the show. I said my goodbyes to her and went to the dimly lit club. I sat in the back as the opening hardcore band blasted through their set. It was somewhere near the end (why is that that the worse bands always seemed to play for the longest time) when I noticed one of the gutter punks in the crowd blew chunks in the pit area. The smell of vomit took over the club, but somehow the moshing went on as the band kept blazing through their set. Soon another pit person had enough and also threw up on the floor.

By now the people of the pit were slipping and sliding in their vomit glory and I think another couple of people puked before the band ended. Oblivion knew no matter how we played when it was our turn all we would hope was that no one would puke over our music.

Another Toronto time a year or so later had us playing this music fest. Now my stand point on music fest, especially punk ones, is that they get boring really fast. Not all, but most. So anyhow we had learned on the drive up from some classic rock station near Detroit, that David Lee Roth was recording some songs with Van Halen again.

Now picture a man in his 40's wearing the smallest set of blue jean shorts that a man should wear. You could see hairy ass cheek if you looked. Unfortunately, we all looked. This long haired metal/punk guy was the emcee of the festival and Pete lets him know of the info and he announced us as the American band with some news about Van Halen. It was the best intro announcement we would ever get. And probably one of the few times that when we played a show that they didn't mess up our name. Oblivion is an easy name and a word in the dictionary, but somehow when it came time for some emcee to say it, it became 'oblivan', "oblivs", "obligated", "obituaries", oh rock and roll.

We closed out the year with another show at the Metro and helping Chuck clean up a place that would become the bar Club Foot. Major publications like Spin magazine would declare thanks to Green Day's *Dookie* record, that 1994 was the year that punk broke, but for us 1995 would be the year everything changed.

The year would start off full force with our Kiss tribute band KISSS. Keep in mind the real Kiss wouldn't reunite back to the original guys until 1996, so in '95 people were hungry for people wearing the makeup. We would rehearse at the Underdog Records loft and during one practice a guy on the street below ran home and got a Kiss record. He ran back to show his devotion by screaming up to the loft at us and holding the record up. Kiss didn't have fans after all, they had an army! After a show at the Fireside Bowl, I crashed on a couch at the Underdog loft. I woke up the next day and peeled my sweaty body off the couch, and noticed an almost perfect outline of the cat man make up left on the cushions. It was silly how quickly the KISSS thing took off. The audience soon took it way more seriously than we did. We got offers for shows out of state and it became silly as for all four of us, it was just a dumb and fun idea that went too far. I did enjoy finally singing as I got to do "Hard Luck Woman." I was thankful the guys didn't laugh when I first tried singing at practice. I could always blame the fact that I was trying to do the drugged out version of the Kiss drummer. We even had an indie movie about tribute bands come and film us bowling before a Fireside Bowl show. It all was amusing and served its purpose well of allowing us four to let loose a little. It allowed me to pretend to be a rock star while trying to be one as well, if that makes sense? It also allowed Scott a side job in being our pyro guy, which only consisted of lighting a few sparklers during our version of "Rock and Roll All Nite." I would laugh my ass off as he streaked across the small stages lighting up sparklers. The joke of making fun of such an enormous stage show with such a small one, was never lost on me.

I was always out, going to shows, or record shopping. I even finally had a leather jacket with both band's names on it as well. I had seen Joe Queer when he came to town with his leather jacket with The Queers across it and thought it was sort of cool and cheesy at the same time to walk around with your own band's name on your jacket. My brother gave me his jacket after he outgrew it so I already had the leather I just needed the names. I gave it to Joey Vindictive's wife Jenny, who I would talk to as I shopped for music at their store The Dummyroom. After I got it back all painted with Oblivion on the top and The Bollweevils across the bottom, I was just asking for it now for people to come up to me even more at shows and ask if I was in either bands and when our next shows were? Or for people to yell "You suck!" at me when they thought either of the bands were sell outs for playing poppy style punk since Green Day had ruined everything in their lives by going to a major label.

In February, we jumped on a portion of the annual No Empathy winter tour that took us past the college towns of Champaign, Illinois and Carbondale to the great state of Texas once again. The Smoking Popes came along as well and were rumored to be signing to a major label which would turn out to be true as they would soon sign with Capitol records and have their Johann's Face sappy but excellent pop punk release *Born to Quit* come out again on a major label.

This time we were going about as far south in that big ass state as we could with playing in Corpus Christi. A guy there had gotten our records and had a lot of his friends listen to them. The crowd response was so good that as we drove towards home we all mentioned how cool it would be to do this full time. Now after being in this band for 6 years at this time my dream of overnight rock star had long but faded. I was more realistically looking at it being a band that could fill up the bigger halls in Chicago and hopefully draw a few hundred people on the road. Make a blue collar living doing something that I loved and something that I didn't dread doing day to day. We told ourselves we would set a date later in the year and go for it. I was already dropping out of school and thinking that UPS wouldn't be the career I really wanted anyway. A mid-day shift opened up at work and after working so many nights, it felt good to be able to hang out with friends and book more shows having evenings free. This also put a strain on my school as the vast majority of the classes I needed to finish were only offered during the hours I now was at work. I told myself that I would take a few semesters off and between being a band guy go back and finish up. Not doing what it took to complete my degree would turn out to be one of my few regrets in life. Since I now had nights free I would D.J. with this guy I knew from booking shows in Elgin named Brian Peterson. We would do a free for all night every Tuesday at Chuck's bar, Club Foot. It instantly took off as the place to be to drink and listen to these two dumbass D.J's play all kinds of music. I would try to play as much local punk as I could while Brian P. would throw on the most outrageous sounding bands to irritate the crowd, who often ate it up.

One night I told him about Oblivion's plans to go full time and he asked if he could book our tour since he was also booking a lot of shows for the Bowling Alley place called Fireside Bowl.

Fireside Bowl had also become a second home to me. Somehow a local punk kid asked this bowling alley on Fullerton Avenue in Chicago if they could have a few bands set up in the space where people usually looked for shoes and play a benefit show. Word got out that this bowling alley was willing to have all age punk shows and it seemed overnight the legendary Fireside Bowl was born. The owner Jim and I got along very well. We both loved Chicago history along with talking like these heavy Chicago accented characters B-Ice (me) and J-Crew (him.) Stupid things we did to pass the time away.

Fireside Bowl would of course go on to gain national attention as the Chicago place to play when everyone was trying to place Chicago as the new hip place to be since we had a few mid 90's hits come from Chicago acts like Liz Phair, Smashing Pumpkins and Urge Overkill. Even though none of those acts played Fireside Bowl, but national press usually never get anything right until well after the fact anyway. As in by the time the masses hear about some movement, it is usually on its way out.

I gave Brian the month of October to set sail across the US of A. That spring Oblivion would take a few weeks off and on to record our second full length for Johann's Face Records. We all thought that the label would soon explode as to me it was Chicago's answer to the very popular Sub Pop records out West. We had Not Rebecca, Apocalypse Hoboken, The Smoking Popes back catalog, as well as No Empathy. Everyone was at the top of their game and turning out some decent rock music. Since I was busy with Bollweevil activities, Pete and Scott handled the final mix down of the record in one of Chicago's hottest days of the year. A summer that saw over 700 hundred heat related deaths where the hottest day reached 106 degrees. I later heard how Pete froze a giant three liter bottle of RC cola and placed it between his legs to put up with the heat. The solo small air unit had to be turned off so they could listen very closely to the tape. The boys soldiered on as they mixed what would become *Shoot Me A Waco*.

Waco was not a political themed record by any means, rather we took the title from the tour of the Dr. Pepper museum we had on tour. Our guide told us that in the old days if you wanted a Dr. Pepper cola you would ask the barkeep to "Shoot You A Waco."

That phrase stuck in our minds and with that phrase we told the artist who did our first record Marcus to go ahead and find a photo that would fit in. We all thought with songs like "Bob and Weave", "Actress" and Scott's song "Anavrin" (Nirvana spelt back words) and a slightly cleaner production that even featured horns on "Do Me" that this would be our form of a pop record. So what better way than to have a picture of a kid drinking a cold pop (or soda or cola for you non Chicago people) on the brightly colored cover. I flirted with the idea of finally shooting a video for "Bob and Weave", but we had little free time. I always thought the concept of three skinny white boys coming out onto the Showtime at the Apollo stage and having this inner city African American crowd just loudly boo and throw stuff at us, would be a great concept for a video. At the end they would finally beat our asses and the clip would be a takeoff on all the generic band plays in front of crowd that normally wouldn't like them, but through the power of their latest single, worlds are brought together crap that was overused in videos.

The record also featured some of Pete's best song structured in "Opera Night." Scott was often in a tough spot, as Pete and I would push at times towards a simpler melodic guitar solo of sorts much like guitarist Jughead did for Screeching Weasel. But often he played the more intricate solo which often in punk you don't often hear. On the first track "We Hate Reruns", the solo he came up with is perfect in its form. For his overall song writing, I really like a lot of songs he did later when he gave me a tape of songs for his post Oblivion band The Knobs. I wish we had a few of those songs as I was never too big into tunes like Ann, although that song did feature Tom from Not Rebecca, which was cool. I always felt like if Oblivion had gone longer we would have had more guest musicians on our records as well as really expanded our musical output in the studio.

With our silly stage antics sometimes and song lyrics, I always thought Pete never got the recognition he deserved as a song writer. No one in punk really gets too much credit for writing songs it seems. I would watch him as he could listen to a song, any song even punk stuff from Pegboy to Screeching Weasel and sit at a piano at his former college (at this time both Pete and Scott had graduated college) and play it. His choice of different tempos and moods in this one song amazed me. When he would come to practice with a tape of a song he recorded I would usually keep the drum beats he played on some cheesy keyboard setting as the structure for what I would eventually play, as we heard the same things in the song. Scott also did a great job with "Do Me" on this record which is one of his stronger songs. I was never a big fan of all of his songs to be honest, as I felt some were on the lighter edge of what we should be playing as a harder rock band. But since I couldn't come up with anything better, I just shut my mouth and played them as fast as he would let me. We all had our turn to play something on the record's closer "Day Job" as I even played guitar on it as a joke since I sucked at it, but I got to live out my dream as no one really dreams to be a drummer, but everyone wants to be a guitar player or singer.

Shoot Me A Waco came out in September and sold just as good as the first one did at our record release show. Now mind you Johann's Face was only pressing around 1,000 CD's and 500 LPs, but to us it was good enough. It was also good enough to keep my youthful music dream alive, even with feeling older by the minute in such a young scene.

The crowd at the official Chicago release was so big that the Fireside Bowl which would somehow hold well over 400 or more kids (the legal capacity was around 140 or so) had to turn away more than 100 people. We had other release shows lined up in Champaign and Rockford, but that didn't help console those not getting in. After parties were often held at Club Foot. It was at Club Foot that after searching all over for my next girlfriend, I would met this pretty college preppy type looking blond girl sitting with the younger of the Texas sisters who went to Pete's former college. Even though I was into the punk scene, the girls out of the scene were the ones I was always attracted to. I really liked the odds stacked up against me for some strange reason.

It was an almost instant hit it off thing which was dumb as I was soon leaving for a month to go on the road. Speaking of dumb, to get in shape for the road we somehow thought of a bright idea while playing a local gymnasium in the suburbs. (Again punk shows were held anywhere.) After every song we celebrated by taking a lap around the track on the floor. Our sets would usually only be around a quickly played 10 to 12 songs thankfully as after about song five or six it was taking us three, more than a few minutes to get around this damn gymnasium.

We around then also came up with our alter ego band Oblivion U.K. which basically we did when we were bored with our regular set since we played so often. Oblivion U.K. was just us playing our songs plus a few more covers in horrible English accents during our between song banter with the crowd.

My favorite Oblivion U.K. moment came when at a Metro show we decided to come out with the Texas girls playing the guitars (which they couldn't) and then have Pete and Scott come out as mad Englishmen as Oblivion U.K. and insult everyone. In order to do this to the full effect we made the poor

Metro door guy go upstairs and walk out to the huge marquee sign and add the letters U and K after our name. It was epic.

Things were often strange, as we never really knew what would take place at our shows. We came up with a song list but often also had dumb themes along with it. Pete and I would talk about what we were going to do and wear often leaving Scott out of it in the beginning for no other reason than just wanting to do something that would be entertaining to both he and the crowd. We were about to take this little entertaining punk act on the road, as Brian soon told us he booked a solid four weeks of shows from houses to clubs to everything in between.

Scott had told his hot dog stand job so long, and Pete had left his gig at Home Juice. I gave UPS my notice and then was thinking of how to tell my mother who would be coming back from her six month Florida stay soon. She wasn't that upset when I dropped out of college as my mother never expected me to go very far in school. She thought the military or blue-collar world was where my futureless planning ass would end up. As she pulled into the driveway I told her and she actually took it well, but informed me that I would have to pay 100 bucks to rent out a small portion of the basement between the cat litter and pool table as my big sister was going to move back into the house with her kid and his father to help out and keep an eye on the place since my mom was only living there 6 months out of the year.

I was excited to go and by now you know how all The Bollweevils took to my touring full time with Oblivion. But before that heart break I had to leave my new full time serious girlfriend behind. Only a jackass like me falls in love before setting off into the great unknown. No more rock and roll sex parties for me (well there were really none anyway).

I was a taken man. And with the Sex part of Sex Drugs and Rock and Roll out of the picture for the road all I had since drugs were never my thing was Rock and Roll.

We purchased a van with all our band savings. We all lucked out with all our folks being cool enough to still let us all live at home. We once tossed around the idea of all living in a small apartment in the Chicago suburb Melrose Park, IL but thought we needed to keep our cost of living as low as possible to even try to make this dream work. I went to our booker Brian's place and grabbed the piece of paper of all the contacts we had to call. It was then I saw that he had us booked for six weeks plus and that some of the shows just listed a town and a note beside it that said "call me when you get there." What the fuck had we done?

The shows on our first major tour went good enough. A lot weren't that well attended but we didn't expect them to be, as we knew we weren't the type of band that had a lot of hype to us or that one could easily classify us. We were like the average looking girlfriend that had to grow on someone instead of the hottie that got the instant attention.

On the tour we played New York in which we met some girls that worked at Delia's catalog. Delia's was and is a clothing retail place aimed at skinny teenage girls. It was nice of them to come out as in the big apple our show was the place not to be I guess, as the crowd was only a handful of people. We thought that maybe they were pissed about our song "Looking Through The Delia's Catalog", but they actually loved that we mentioned the new clothing companies name. We later got a tour of the warehouse where they actually let Pete work the phones to take an order or two while Scott and I walked down the panty isle and took pictures like we were touring the Great Wall of China or something.

Jill's face from Delia's would later be featured on our split cd with Man Dingo.

Life on the road consisted of us getting lunch (or as we called it our meal of the day) at Taco Bell, arriving to the show early and sitting out in front of the venue or house and then loading in and having the small crowd ask us about Chicago and punk rock. We often drove out after the show to get a head start on the next day. None of us had drinking or drug problems, so it was easy to do. We all had the same hard work ethic when it came to being on the road. We took showing up and loading in fast seriously and wanted to show the promoter in each town that we meant business. We also had this thing if we had small drives where right before our last song, we would ask for a place to stay. You would be surprised at how often people opened up their house to some skinny strange band. As musicians we became tight as we could play the songs almost on auto pilot. To prevent things from becoming monotonous, we would change the set every show to keep mixing things up.

We celebrated our first Thanksgiving on the road with the band Cletus. Cletus and Minnesota's The Strike were bands that Johann's Face were now releasing singles with as well as soon working on future full lengths. Cletus was led by singer Johnny Puke. The word on Puke was that he knew the one and only crazy punk rocker G.G. Allin, and was with him during his last moments. Talk about crazy punk street cred. Johnny and Pete were always an interesting personality mix in the same room. I always liked Mr. Puke, and the band Cletus was power pop punk to its finest. I thought how could Johann's not become the next big indie label with all these bands? Oblivion seemed to be at the right place and during the right time, so hopefully things would start going our way. What would be better than making it semi-big on your own terms on a record label full of bands you liked that consisted of people who were your friends. We tried to promote the label as much as we could on tour.

Cletus spoiled us with plenty of turkey and also plenty of porn viewing capabilities... Nothing like being introduced to sweet potato pie and Savannahs back catalog all on the same night! It seemed like just when sleeping in the van and poorly attended shows were getting to us, we would have a great night of a good show and a nice floor to refuel our little rock engines.

That first tour was also lonely for me as I was having fun but couldn't wait at times to get back to my new girlfriend. She took the train down to see our last two shows in Carbondale and Champaign. At this point I should mention my history with Champaign and Carbondale two Illinois college towns.

Remember when you are a kid and your school has some field trip to the zoo or to learn how candy is made, well this was how I approached shows on the road. Now of course everyone has a different definition of a road show. For me it was anything over 60 minutes to get there. And then a tour was any combo of shows that lasted more than a week. As we booked many the two to three day weekend warrior thing, but it wasn't the same as touring. I liked to venture into new places, and I really loved to venture into college towns. These two were my favorite. Not sure if it was some deep rooted embarrassment or insecurities for not being able to go away to college, or what brought out the wacky side a little more in these towns.

Oblivion would at times instigate the crowd by playfully taunting the audience. Some bands yell at the crowd to mosh or to jump or whatever, but we could care less what they did as long as they came to the shows. At out of town shows Pete would say that no matter how much you didn't liked us the difference between us and you is that we get to leave this shit hole tomorrow and you all have to live here. Most of the time the people got the joke, but every so often you got a can or shoe tossed up your way with some boos. We seemed to enjoy that just as much as a crazy crowd surfing pit. What we wouldn't put up with is a bunch of people just half ass standing there acting bored, and thankfully we didn't have to worry about that too much. I often wonder how we would have handles this new thing of everyone sticking their phones up to take a photo and then texting each other during the show.

Champaign crowds were always accepting of us even when we were insulting them. We usually played to a pack hall or house. The best was when we played early enough for me to get paid and check out The Jesus Lizard and catch David Yow's boot in my face a few times. Ah, The Jesus Lizard.

At one early Carbondale show back when we did the weekend warrior thing, I remember coming back to this friend's dorm room. We all decided to spend the night in town and leave the next morning, so I was trying to find a place to crash other than the van. This girl's roommate came in and started to go through her closet. I saw her old high School plaid skirted uniform and somehow after a few beers I found myself on the streets in her dress. I found an orange on the ground and thought it would be nice to throw it. I tossed it up towards a Frat house just as the door opened and the orange rolled past the people coming out. Some big guy took this as a threat from the skinny multicolored hair kid rocking the school girl outfit and takes off after me. Luckily I wasn't drunk enough to haul ass and loose this mammoth in the bushes a block away. I somehow slowly remembered my way back to the dorms and for my reward of going out in the dress, I got to snuggle her roommate for a few hours until the van pulled up and we had to go. Snuggling is what I did when I was too shy to make the first move of a big ole kiss. I was such a wuss.

Another time, Oblivion shared a show with Apocalypse Hoboken. The house show was packed and almost everyone there was wasted on something. The guys who owned the house paid us with a nitrous oxide tank. The party had one they were using to make whip it's from, and then he gave one to Hoboken which Todd Pott gladly took over and also to us. Pete and Scott being smarter than I knew what it was. I wasn't sure if like Helium it would make your voice go up an octave or two. I found myself in the corner of this basement party with my own tank. I took a hit then had this quick brain freeze sort of rush. I did a few more and it all turned into a head ache. Some guy came over and told me to be careful, as it will screw up with your oxygen somehow. All I remember is that my curiosity got the best of me and after a while with this tank and alcohol I staggered up the flight of stairs which probably took an hour or so but who noticed a messed up drummer on a staircase anyway.

I got outside somehow and passed out on the lawn. I awoke to find people asking me if I was getting a ride with the band or not. I told them to tell the boys I can find another way home. I remember Gar taking me back to Chicago as he was also having an out of body experience. Oblivion's song Gar just may have been written about this episode or not. Gar had so many to choose from but a lightweight like me soon realized my limits. Ah college towns.

Carbondale was also the home of the Lost Cross house. One of those places you could describe as saying "punk as fuck." It was always an amazing time to play this packed punk house's basement. Picture the Animal House but filled with smelly drunk punks. One show ended in a riot, which spilled out onto the street with cops and campus security alike. Shows at Lost Cross would always be something to talk about at the end of the tour.

After these two college gigs we came home not knowing what would be our next move. I had been working and going to school for what seemed like forever and now here I was with only one responsibility. Oblivion. I sat amongst all my junk squeezed in between the pool table and cat litter boxes in the basement of the house and oddly enough was happy. The same spot in the basement that years before I set up my cardboard barrier full of rock posters, I was now sitting as a full time musician. Just a really badly paid one. To make a little money to take my new girlfriend out, I would get some tips from DJ'ing at club foot on the packed Tuesday nights as well as on select Wednesdays I was the world's worst bartender at the new home of Chicago punk, The Fireside Bowl. We ended that year of change 1995, with a show at the fireside of which I remember nothing. Not from too much partying mind you, just from me now being too damn old to remember everything.

We kicked off the next year 1996 with a show at Pete's former college. Gone were the days of all our friends attending the school, but hello were the days of my girlfriend being able to convince the student union to let us play and to pay us well. After taking two years off from hanging out in the creepy hallways it was an odd feeling to be back amongst the crazy Catholics at Rosary College. They made us change our promos for the show after they felt *Shoot Me A Waco* was named in some honor of the massacre. Why oh' why can't people think of Dr. Pepper when they hear the word Waco? It would be one of the only times we ever listened to any form of censorship.

We were entering another time. Our older crowd that had been there since the start was now opting to stay at home for most of our shows. One person actually called me and told me they liked it better when no one came to see us. How strange indeed, but I also could understand what he meant.

A week later on January 26th we headlined the Metro for the first time. It was a milestone for sure. From going to playing bad suburban metal clubs on weekdays and getting rejection letters from the Metro just a few years before, to headlining there and on a Friday night of all nights.

That February, we went out on the Johann's Face annual tour again which lasted all month. The shows like our previous tour were all hit and miss. But with Mark, along with singing in No

Empathy and running the label, had booked this tour so it gave our booker Brian time to work on another little trip for us.

You got some curious people seeking out these bands from Chicago, as no one knew who would be the next big breakout story of the scene. There were some shows where we doubted we would ever break out of anything as we would go to the promoters place like in Shreveport, LA for instance and often find the promo material that Johann's sent out still sitting there. When this kid finally was awake enough he made some copies of a last minute flyer and 'Pete, Scott and I hit the local college to hand some around at any kid who looked like he might be interested in going out that night. When a club is open you obviously can see their clientele, but at daytime where do you go? Our two choices were often the local college and the mall. The turn out that night actually wasn't so bad for a show that was promoted just hours beforehand. To break up the boredom we would announce ourselves as various major label bands like Boston, The Doors, The Who etc.... as a node to the news that previous Johann's artist the Smoking Popes had indeed signed with big bad Capitol Records and we hoped they would enjoy a mega success that would get people interested in seeking out their history which might just include people checking out other bands on their former label. Kind of like when Green Day broke and a select amount of people cruised through the Lookout Records catalog.

I came home from that tour and rested a few hours before getting on a plane to show off my new girlfriend to my mom in Florida. Since she looked like a pretty college girl, I hoped that my mom wouldn't have lost all hope to me yet. Meeting my girlfriend's family was another story, as there is no way to say you're in a rock band to answer their question of "what do you do." As any scrawny kid with two-toned hair and a leather jacket would have any other answer to that question anyway.

I finally spent a week or two home which consisted of me doing what I could for tips. I wrote a bunch of music reviews for the local publications as well as jumped into the studio to record some various songs for compilation CD's. Since we had two full lengths out we were now recording a few songs here and there for people that were asking. I also was hoping since neither of the two CD's were breaking us that maybe someone filming a movie would want a song for their soundtrack. Something had to happen for my musical dream to come true. I was getting delirious and desperate. I got a letter from a video game company asking if they could use the intro from our song "School" in a game. I wrote back asking for more information and also telling them I was surprised they even wrote as if they just stole the music who would ever know. I never got a reply. Somehow I think there is a kid playing a retro 90's video game with some Zelda like character roaming around a castle with the bass riff for "School" looping over and over as he collects some wild berries or some shit for mega points. Oh well.

We went right back on the road for a short two week tour in March and April. What was once the longest we could go out for due to work and school was now considered a short tour. I was noticing when we came home we would split the earnings into four. One slice going into the band fund to pay for studio time or to make shirts, and the other thirds going to us individually. As cheap as I had made my life with just basic insurance policy and eating only when necessary it was rough. It was a contrast of playing well attended local shows to the crap shoot of touring with the only common theme being the fact that I was broke all the time. Oblivion had a Metro show lined up and the local Chicago station WXRT wanted us to promote it. Local punk was growing and no one wanted to seem uncool and on the out, so all these media chances be it local radio or the Sun Times or Tribune didn't want to be left out.

I took the call to be on air at my girlfriend's dorm room. One of the jockeys asking how it felt to be doing so well and to be able to tour and play places like the Metro. I laughed as here I was doing this radio interview while starving to death, skinny, drop out, and broke living mostly in my girlfriend's tiny dorm room eating my favorite sandwich of two slices of white bread, with some smashed up Jays chips with a taco bell sauce packets squeezed into it. Yeah, I was living the dream all right, but I was grateful for still being in a band when it seemed a lot of the bands we came up with like Lunkhead, and 8 Bark all had already called it quits. And I was totally appreciating being in a band that at the time had enough people interested in it to play a place with a real sound system and stage like the Metro.

For instance one time I came up with the idea at a Metro show in front of a thousand people that because it was the holidays it might be funny to announce to the crowd that holidays is time for spending with your family and then plant a slightly too long to be normal kiss on someone that I would announce to be my sister. Granted this would not be a joke in the south, but just another concert. But since this was in Chicago where we have many choices who to go with, I thought it might be a little funny. So my girlfriend at the time asked her little sister to play the part of my sister. Which is still kind of odd if you think about it. Unbeknownst to me she told her to really plant one on me to turn my joke on me and to slip the old tongue in, as she knew I really wasn't a fan of public affection. So the Metro announcer announces Oblivion, stage lights go up, and before going behind my drums I walk center stage arm in arm with this skinny blond girl and continue with my joke of telling the crowd that holidays are a time to reunite with your family and then lean in for a kiss...so I get grabbed into this tongue festival, shocking me a little as the crowd goes awkwardly ape shit and we start our set.

Sure enough after the show this guy came up to me and asked me all concerned and a little bummed out that he never knew I had a little sister and that she was cute. Nothing about the fact that why the hell did you just make out with her or anything, but rather is she available, wondering if we were an item or something. I waited a few minutes being explaining to him that I had no younger sister and he was free to ask out anyone he wanted to.

Another Metro fiasco was later during my time as a preschool instructor. After cleaning out the classroom I had assorted Barney (the annoying purple dinosaur) and Toy Story plush toys I was going to toss. Instead I put them in my truck. Later that week as I was unloading my drums at the Metro I noticed the stuff figures and thought these need to go down my pants. So as we took the stage I ran back down to the dressing room and put on my tight ass fake leather pants and started stuffing these stuffed animals along my belt line. I should share this back story with you first. Joe Shanahan was the big time and might still be Metro guy. He discovered the Smashing Pumpkins and has friends in high places and all that. His first exposure to me (besides those cheesy rejection letters we got years before) was telling me to put my pants on as I was the last in line of the three Oblivion members up the stairs and out to the stage to hit members of Apocalypse Hoboken with some foam bats during their fine song "Microscopic."

So now we fast forward a few months to the Toy Story gig. So there I am with the pants filled with various characters and I walk past none other than the owner Joe himself. I overheard him asking the security guard "who was playing" as he was surprised the early all age show was packed. After the hulk like guard proclaimed "Oblivion" he said, "I just don't get the appeal of that band." I smiled as I ran up the last few steps and out the stage, and always wanted to use that quote on a flyer or something but never got around to doing so.

Oblivion, or mostly Pete rather, always had some kind of interesting idea for a themed performance. During the fireside years we played there too much and were always looking for a new way to entertain ourselves. One night was a dinner/show night. Pete got a table out, placed it center stage and ordered a crap load of KFC. We ate in between songs until the grease from the chicken started to get all over us, and my drum sticks slipped out my hands and almost poked this poor girls eyes out who was sitting on the stage. It also was hard to play full speed with a gut full of processed mashed potatoes and biscuits.

Oblivion had this thing for the USA theme. Much of the punk scene was anti-nationalist or something. Not really proud to be anything and hated politics and all that. We embraced the stupidity as well as excellence of America in all its glory. We would sometimes use intro songs or themes before we took the stage. The most entertaining was when we used Elvis's "American Trilogy." As the King sang in "The Battle Hymn of the Republic" the words "Glory, glory, hallelujah" we would take the stage. The best was doing it on the road when we would have a small crowd of maybe ten to twenty people and we would be waiting to take the stage (often a wooden platform just inches high) by standing just next to it still in full view of the small audience. A Spinal Tap moment for sure, and we loved it.

My favorite of the stage antics was our White Trash party again at the Fireside bowl. We all wore some kind of shirts and sweat pants with American flags and other such items on it. We scattered chips, junk food, and snacks all over the stage. During a in between song bit, I asked my girl to come up on stage as she had gotten the wrong flavor of potato chips. Something that I am sure in some trailer park has actually taken place. As she approached the stage I reprimanded her telling her she knew the flavor I liked, as she was apologizing in a sort of Miss Elizabeth to the Macho Man kind of way I "hit" her over the head with the bag of chips. What I actually did was slightly graze the top of her head as I tossed the already ripped open bag all over the stage to make that dramatic effect. The show went on and all was well, then after the show I had this fairly large guy block my way as I was carrying my drums out telling me it ain't cool to hit girls. So like the bag of chips to my drunk girlfriend, it all just went over his head.

After our first few tours in 1996, I realized that what little money I was bringing home $100-200 was being spent too fast on my rent and auto insurance and at times food and I was having to dip into my UPS money to survive. I was living the cheapest of a life I could possibly do other than be homeless.

My sister, who had moved into the house, felt sorry for me. I told her we could do ok on the road with just getting by but that it's when you have a few weeks at home, it was hard to do anything but be broke. She offered me a job at the day care she was working at. I would cook and after I got a cdl, I would drive the small bus with kids to field trips and stuff. It wasn't that I wanted to be around snotty little kids, but 8 an hour seemed like a million bucks to these starving musicians. And it seemed as soon as the brats at work pissed me off, it was time to go back onto the road. We went away for most of May and June. We were now keeping some of our cloths in the van. We also stopped hanging around each other so much when we weren't on the road. It was indeed the end of another era. Gone were the days of us three pulling up into a party or show and hoping we could make some friends with our goofy antisocial but wacky antics. We were now forming our own circle of friends as to not grow too tired of one another. My circle was very small consisting of usually just myself roaming around Chicago's Northside going to Reckless Records or back in the suburbs listening to CD's in my girlfriend's tiny dorm room. On the road Pete would wake up early and have his walks around strange towns, which usually ended at some greasy spoon to get breakfast. Scott was an amazing sleeper and I often would get up just after Pete and look through people's music collection if we were staying at someone's house. I also liked to explore towns to pass the time, or search around in the hopes for a working pay phone to call back home. We had been in some towns more than once now so we had hangouts in each town.

The student unions at various big colleges were always a place to find an arcade to pass the time as well as Pete had no problems with asking people walking towards the garbage cans who had left overs on their tray if he could finish them off. Scott and I also had this stupid thing we did usually at truck stops very late at night in which we would go into stalls in empty bathrooms and make the most unusual pooping sounds with our mouths to make the other laugh as we did our business. One time as we were getting obscenely louder and louder I quietly slipped out my door and stood at the entrance of the bathroom. This big trucker guy walks in as Scott was really letting go his version of the world's biggest fart (now truckers are used to microwave truck stop burritos so they hear all kinds of sounds). The trucker turns to the stall and asks, "You ok in there boy."

I almost had to go back into the bathroom as I was peeing my pants in laughter as I could just picture the look on Scotts face realizing he wasn't alone with me. Three traveling slap happy dumb boys. We went back out in April and May. In June we shared a bill in Eglin at "The Big Show" with the Bollweevils. As stated before, it was sort like watching an old girlfriend friend sleep with someone new. It would be the only time I ever saw them after ditching me. Besides touring we were doing a lot of long weekend shows where we could venture to places like Wisconsin, Minnesota, and Ontario, Canada without getting too burnt out and allowing us to come home and work our odd jobs for cash... We were also coming home to entertain our friends with road stories. Some of my favorites from some interesting places were:

Sometimes on tour we would bring some poor soul along, or pick someone up. Gar who worked for the Johann's Face Record Company, was one of those people. We picked him up in Nashville and brought him on the southern portion of our East coast/South tour. After a show we went to one of those all you can eat stuff your fat ass type places. We were talking about other bands and making fun of people, you know, your general tour topics. We all had colorful language and even though we were all college educated, our vocab never left the gutter. Being in the bible belt, I am sure we, well I know we were offending some, as the table next to us leaned over and said in a thick Southern accent "We appreciate you boys not using language like that."

Somehow they got lost in the translation in our northern city minds and all we could do was to thank the couple for noticing and we went back on to our talk. We actually thought that how they worded it they were expecting maybe more swearing from us odd looking gents and that they were thanking us for not being so over the top, when in all actuality they were asking us to stop the swearing.

Up north it would have been a more direct to the point "Hey fuckheads, there are kids here, stop swearing."

Gar was something, and I am glad to know him. Pete wrote the classic "Gar" after that short tour with him helping sell our shirts and records. Nothing like playing Athens, Georgia and being heckled by your own shirt salesmen who took the bands drink tickets (not that we used them very much anyway) and had himself a party. After that show we had to pack up everything around his passed out self in our van. I guess I had a greater tolerance towards the drunk or stoned, but he was weighing on Pete and Scott who expected maybe more help on this tour and not someone to baby sit. If you listen to the opening of rock games and you hear a drunken Harry Caray impression (a famous Chicago Cubs baseball broadcaster), well that is good ol' Gar. We all spent the night taking our turns saying the crudest things in our Harry Caray voices. I recorded that after the night of the southern buffet now that I think of it. Good times.

By now you are getting the sense that life on the road for Oblivion wasn't all sex drugs and rock and roll. It was thinking about sex, Taco Bell, and rock and roll, but spending a lot of time bored sitting in a van, waiting for the show to happen.

The after parties were seldom attended as usually no one would invite us, so we ended up sleeping at the kid's house who wanted to stay up all night and watch horror movies or ask us if we knew any bands on Fat Wreck Chords. But let's not think it all was G rated.

Sometimes strange things just find you. And it is witnessing or taking part in these strange events that will warp your idea of a good time. I can't tell you how many times I went or still go to a party and since nothing really odd is happening, I just kind of get bored. I would remember towns and states by events that took place. I would be able to remember the highways one needed to get from place to place. I was becoming a road dog as they say. I didn't know it so much then, but I was having some of the best times of my life in various states.

Arkansas. We never wanted to drive far between shows as that wasted whatever little money you may have made. As well as everyone deserves a good show. It's not your fault you were born so far away from one of the cool major cities, or states. So you end of playing places like Arkansas. We did a show at a karate school once (punk bands play the darndest places) that got shut down right before we played. The opening bands were all hardcore kid bands that sang about anarchy and not listening to your parents and of course fucking the police or something like that... that is until the actual police showed up and asked the show to stop since the place was not permitted for having concerts or something like that. The crowd and revolutionary bands all broke away faster than you can so no police brutality.

So there we were.

Another fine show that actually went on with us asking the crowd if anyone knew of a place to stay before our last song. Some girls offered and of course I was interested in that given my views that any place a girl offers should be cleaner and have some kind of food involved than some guy. But since these girls were giggly and being flaky, we took to this grungy looking kid who said he had a house...a house. Keep in mind we are in rural Arkansas. So on the way there we got some beer for Gar and kept driving. We went on driving even as we entered the back woods of Arkansas. We all looked out the van windows waiting for the albino looking hillbilly kid from "Deliverance" to start jamming at any moment. One cannot describe the back woods unless you have seen this sight for yourself. We pulled into the less grown weeds area than the other weeds, otherwise known as the driveway. And saw that not only was there a car up on blocks but the kid's house was also a rundown trailer on blocks. Not to judge as staying in a punk house, beggars can't be choosers, we walked in and soon discovered that it wasn't his house but his parents.

He introduced us to his very large mother (picture a gigantic woman in a moo moo at a Walmart and you are getting very close) and his skinny overall wearing father. (Picture any back woods character from a horror movie and again you're close) So we looked at each other and decided to sit down on what furniture they had. The kid yelled at his mother to make some spaghetti for us, but we all (although being very hungry) declined the offer, as we wanted to. His parents then told us it was late and they had work the next day so that we should try to keep it down. No problem from us as we wanted to sleep a few hours and then get the heck out of dodge. It was then as I was sitting in this beaten down chair that I looked past the antenna on the small black and white TV and noticed a door with a large lock bolt on it. The boy told me it was his sister's room. Insert any joke you want about the south and incest and you would probably be close to correct in this situation.

As I took my sleeping spot just inches from Scott in the boys' room just off the living room mind you each room you could probably touch the walls on either side if you spread your arms out like a flying chicken hawk. Scott like me was fully clothed, jacket, shoes, pants on, and all as we wanted no part of our skin to touch this kid's bed. We then heard the boy from the room (trailers have paper thin walls, and this place was no exception) ask if he could try on Gar's leather jacket. The kid proclaimed to Gar that he had always wanted a cool black leather jacket, and the one he was trying on was just the right style. As he slipped it on the kid started frantically yelling "MA...MA! Look, the jacket fits!!!"

"Hey MA!" he yelled several times and finally Ma yelled back to "Shut up!" which had no effect on the kid. Somehow I faded into sleep with in all the commotion of the boy, his nicely fitting jacket and his big mommy. Scott and I got stomachaches as we tried our hardest not to belly laugh at the situation playing out. I awoke and walked into the living room to stretch my legs as I heard a door handle move and this kids sister ran out of her room, past me, and out the door. A cheetah would have had a hard time catching up to her. I just got a glimpse of what looked to be a normal looking teenage girl. Poor girl. Probably was really good at track and wrestling given her situation and all.

Colorado. It seems we could never get a break. We played this club once where the bar area which was separated by some plastic orange fencing served a minor and the cops came in and raided the overcrowded drunk fest as a fight broke out. Nothing like having one cop telling you to hurry up and pack your shit up as another tells you to get the fuck out of the club now! Decisions, decisions. As I walk out onto the street and the guys are packing the van up I had to become a stealth ninja sneaking back and forth to get my drums out during the frenzy of it all.

The next Colorado show would also have fights and cops but at least this time the show kept going on. It was a show that I had to have my dumbest idea yet (even worse than my short lived fire breathing attempt which I burnt my upper lip). I took this plastic Stormtrooper mask and wore it during our first song, which basically stopped any air from coming in. I thought maybe if I only wore it for one song it would seem too gimmicky and I wanted to show the crowd my devotion for the odd and for Star Wars. So I kept it on half of the set until I couldn't see from the sweat in my eyes and the loss of air made me puke my brains out after the show.

Georgia. At times we would talk about what we might wear or a theme of the show, again mostly to entertain us and not the crowd. We took the stage after our friends in Quedelechia (most likely misspelled) and all I saw was this bright white light coming from side stage as Pete walks on stage completely nude as his bass guitar covered his junk up front. Apparently it was his birthday which Scott and I forgot about and he wanted to play a show in his pale birthday suit. I got to see more of Pete that night than I ever wanted but the crowd liked it. The club owners must have been amused as well as no one called the cops for indecent exposure.

Nevada. We had a show lined up just outside of Vegas. Our tour itinerary simply had a guy's name and his address. No club, no other bands listed. We hooked up with the guy and spent the day sleeping on his couch and avoiding the 100 plus weather outside. Nighttime comes and we started driving, and driving, and driving out to the desert. Are we going to be killed mob style? We didn't even win anything at the Casinos. We see plywood lined out on the sand and some small speakers. How punk. We notice a lot of cars starting to come out to this remote spot. We got out of the van and looked around. There was nothing and the bright Vegas lights, we only small specks in the distance. The first band sets up and plays as this huge dust storm blows in. No one can see a thing, and since everyone, besides the band and their girlfriends, are inside their cars...no one hears a thing. We race to the safety of our van and not long after this dusty windblown kid comes stumbling over to our van window and asks us if we want to play next as already cars are leaving this desolated spot. We in a very rare moment actually declined the offer to play and called it a night as we picked sand out of our hair all night.

Oklahoma. Tornado alley is an odd place. The kids there were caught in a mixture of religious values being thrown at them from their parents and also just plain being bored. Spend a week in Tulsa and get back to me if you feel otherwise. We were loading up after an ok show in Oklahoma. The venue was a used car lot and it served its purpose for the kids to all come and witness the freaks from the big city Chicago coming to play punk rock. The kids with the newly dyed hair and the recently bought leather jackets all came to the show that night. I was loading up my drums in the hallway waiting for the outside area to become car free so I could drive the van up. I walked around the hall and saw these three kids hanging out in the back corner laughing it up. I noticed one was a cute young girl, so my interest was held enough to witness something that I have to say is one of the wackiest things I have ever seen on the road. One of the boys kept laughing as the other boy unzipped his pants. The girl got down on her knees (which so far is nothing odd for a backstage event) But then the boy starting peeing on this girl and she acted like it was shampoo and took her hands and mixed it into her shoulder length alternative girl dyed black hair. The other guy started taking pictures and falling over with laughter. (Had this been happening today, this would for sure have been the Facebook post of the day) They noticed me and I said hell as the girl got up and started to dry herself off with her ripped t-shirt. I told them I was just here to load up my drums. They said that we played good tonight (always nice to get a compliment from anyone, even people with pee pee on them) and I walked away not sure if I saw the

downfall of mankind or just some young kids being bored...
Really fucking bored, as piss does not make for a good hair care
product.

Pennsylvania. Driving across the I-80 east bound we got
stuck in a snow storm. It was freezing outside, and there was no
way to see out the window and the highway was littered with
semis and cars pulling to the side of the road to wait out the
storm. We kept driving until our visibility became 0. We pulled
off onto a ramp and then into a truck stop. We pulled the van in
a back spot and basically took all the shirts we brought with us
to sell and dumped them all over us. The three of us spooned
under the sea of shirts in the freezing cold in an attempt to try
to use our body heat to keep us warm and to keep us alive. I
always felt sorry for the kids who bought the shirts from that
tour as they had to smell like three skinny idiots freezing to
death with bad body odor.

Somewhere on the East Coast. We had another fun van time
in which after it died we were stranded. We pushed it into the
first spot on a lane in front of a dealership so they would have
to look at the van since we were blocking traffic. That night I
tried to sleep sitting in the drivers using the steering wheel as a
pillow and rocking back and forth to stay warm.

Virginia. We had a few times where our tours would crisscross
other bands we liked and knew. One band was Pansy Division
who were now doing well on Lookout! Records. We played with
them out on the road once where the club had promoted a
Lookout! Band coming to town since everyone was familiar
with the record label as Green Day's old label. Normal jocks
and locals were coming out (no pun intended) now to the
"punk" shows to be cool and not wanting to be left out. The
guys in Pansy were a great bunch of guys to hang out with and
after we played that night, the college crowd started staggering
in and standing in front of the stage. I agreed to look after their
merchandise as the boys went on stage to play. Scott and Pete

joined them on their very gay version of the Judas Priest song "Breaking the Law." As the song blast through the club, a local guy looks leaves the crowd and walks back to where I was. He looks over the records on the table in front of me. Now Pansy Division had no problem about being an openly gay band as they often had dicks and other man loving items on their record art work. This guy looks over all of it and it was only as they sang "Breaking the Law, The Sodomy Law" he looks at me disgusted and asked if they are some kind of "fag band." I looked at him and said "well, it's all how you take it." The guy called me a "fuckin fag" and left disgusted. I guess the new cool punk scene was ruined for him.

Wisconsin. We played a string of shows in the late 90's with the up and coming and very popular band Alkaline Trio. That band made me jealous. They got hot girls, and large crowds right off the bat it seemed. They would go onto playing big shows and getting record deals while Oblivion would be trapped in the underground obscure category. We had a gig with them in Madison where Scott and I told the college kids walking by that we were actually the secret road crew for U2 and that the band was playing a small surprise show at the hall. We would have our road crew look with having hoodies on and keys jangling from our pockets. Scott also had a small flashlight that helped us fit the image. I had a blast talking to Scott loudly in my pissed off road crew voice about how Bono was a dick and wanted the van parked exactly the way he liked it, and for the amps only brought in a certain way. Most of the kids walking by just thought we were nuts, but we hoped that some would venture on in and we could get off on seeing their disappointed faces once we took the stage. In Green Bay, the Chicago Bears actually had a home game against them the day we drove up. Every toll booth operator kept asking us if we knew it was a Chicago home game as we raced north to Green Bay decked out in our Bear jerseys and hats. We arrived at the hall and the Alkaline guys thought we were nuts as we walked into a local restaurant in our blue and orange jerseys. We all thought we had a good chance of getting our asses kicked before the food made its way to our table. Back at the club, I took to the front of the stage before our set and announced "I heard Green Bay has some of the toughest punks on the planet (insert crowd cheering), well, to me and the boys, you all look like a bunch of pussies!" The crowd, besides one or two kids in the back that loved the taunting, didn't know what to make of us. These punk kids came to the show to get away from the sports mentality happening outside, and here we were throwing it into their faces while wearing some football jerseys.

The only real dangerous times were once in St Louis before a show I was walking around when this guy offered me some discounted merchandise, and as I was walking away, he tried pulling me into the alley possibly to rob me. I slithered away with my skinny self and ran down to where we were playing. From that moment on I always hated St Louis and would ask Brian to book us at other places instead, until I realized I'd rather be jumped in the city, then be bored at some of these remote ass towns in Missouri.

Things can happen anywhere. As I was walking with the Man Dingo drummer in Arizona, we left to go pick up some more people for the show and I continued on what I thought was the road that lead to a convenience store. I turned the corner and some rather large Mexican guys all stopped whatever they were doing and looked at me. It was then I noticed the silver reflection of a gun being pulled out as another asked me to go walk on the other side of the street. I had no problems listening and I wasn't even dumb enough to try out my failed college level Spanish on them. But for the most part the people you met on the road were great. I wish they had easier video capabilities back then as I would have loved to make sort videos of every one and their stories from the kid who talked to me about how hard it would be to come out to his parents (who was a big time politician in Arkansas) or with the state trooper in Louisiana about racism in his line of work, to the magnitude of kids I met where we all shared our love of music and the scene and would often sit for hours discussing the band and players involved. And of course the girls in which I could talk to but not touch, but really they were few and far between, but I still remember some. We seemed to play the Fireside Bowl either right before going on or when we came back from a tour. It was a sure way to make a few hundred bucks. We could have did the popular band thing and pay Chicago only a few times a year or wait to get the opening slot for some big national band, but we very rarely turned down a show. We now knew more than ever how it sucked to go to a town and play in front of 5 people. So if we could draw 100-300 people for a touring band we knew it would mean a lot for them even if playing out so much killed our attempt at having a bigger show for ourselves.

You also had times in which you had to smack yourself in the face to see if you would wake up from this crazy dream. Times where you had to laugh or you would just cry. Time like those in L.A. where we pulled into a city of 3 three and a half million people. I thought ok, well maybe one, one hundredth of them like punk and maybe an eight of those people would want to come out on a Monday night to check out a band from Chicago. Not being a math major, I thought we would get maybe 100 people or so. The opening band plays in front of their crowd and then we take the stage in front of one, ONE SINGLE PERSON. We actually stopped a song midway as he left to get a beer at the bar that was adjacent to the club. When he came back, we started the song up again.

The pay you got also kept you smiling in a state of insanity. One night during a down pour in southern New Jersey we played a show in front of a handful of people. After the show, the bar owner tells us he thought more people would come and that he made no money. We understood and started packing our gear up. He walked and handed us a six-pack. He then realized we only had three band members and took off three of the beers. We all stood there with this blank look on our faces as Scott took the now three-pack and handed it to me. I drank all three and due to my low tolerance, got drunk and laughed at the fact that we saw stop lights in the rain, I was losing it.

Back on the home front, Material Issues vocalist/guitarist Jim Ellison had just killed himself by closing himself in a garage with his moped running. I wondered if any of it had to do with the bands quick rise and fall. I remembered speeding after school to get their debut and supporting them with the other Chicago bands I always wanted to hit it big. They never did, and after this obviously would never have a chance to. It sucked but I could remember the excellent concert I went to at the Metro and have that be my memory of Material Issue instead of a guy checking out way too soon. As depressed as I was about my own situation, I never saw any good in ending it by suicide. There was always something to wait to do, and we had a lot of things I wanted to accomplish before checking out the rock and roll way, which of course is in a plane accident.

We again went out for most of July and August. We were playing so much that our hands and fingers knew what we wanted them to do as our minds wandered to other things during shows. The goofiness was at an all-time slap happy high. We started taking the stage to Elvis's "American Trilogy" and wearing these sleeveless American flag shirts. It was Americana at its punk worse. We did a tour with t-shirts with big "O"'s on them. We also took to naming our tours. After seeing one bad St Louis band kick a microphone over (in which during our set after them we lined up some chairs from the crowd and gently knocked them over), we called a tour in honor of that night the brutality to furniture tour.

I was doing my best of trying to stay awake during bartending, DJ'ing, and of course my so-called job in the weeks I was home but it was hard. I was wasting away just during the summer tours and as soon as we came home on August 10th we learned Brian P. was putting us back on the road on the 20th for over four weeks well into September. On the road I had my cranky times. I remember telling Scott I was going to kill him more than once while waiting in a hot van (we didn't have air or heat) for a show promoter to come home in southern California. I was losing it, and I often wondered why this music dream had to be so fucking hard. All I wanted was a living, I didn't need the riches of fame and MTV, I just wanted to get by. I would have looked up and cursed the stars but instead all I saw was the dirty blue fabric ceiling of our old van.

Right now a lot of those shows are a blur, and even back then, days seem to fade into days, from one town to the next, but there is always something that stands out. Unfortunately in September 1996, it wasn't a good thing. One memorable incident would put us to the test. We were warned at the beginning of the tour that this bigger local band in New Orleans made it their gimmick to torture the opening band, which included making fun of them after their set. We made fun of audiences, but we really didn't want to be the butt of some lame rock bands joke. On a previous tour out west we spent the day watching some middle of the road circus acts at Circus Circus in Vegas. People juggling, hot middle-aged ladies in tight skirts handing magicians their props, and of course clowns. There was this one gymnastic trapeze act we laughed at every time they came up which was often as we spent hours there to try to stay out of the outside heat. Sometimes Vegas can feel like the surface of the sun inside a microwave.

Back at this gig in New Orleans, we thought if we could be so outrageous we would force the closing band to be embarrassed to even mention us. Thus getting out of the whole them making fun of us, as no one makes fun of people making fun of everything. So we called ourselves the fabulous Razzilio brothers (never to be pronounced or spelled the same way twice) and in between songs we would yell and clap and I would stand on my drum stool, like it was a tight rope or balance a drum stick in my hands as Scott and Pete would clap and yell and do some gymnastic stances. We must have looked like idiots as the few times I glanced up at the crowd they were looking at us though their pretentious beer glasses and their mouths open. Needless to say the band didn't mention us once. Not a fucking word.

So after that show, we leave and Pete had a friend who lived somewhat in town. We had a decent drive the next day so we were going to do a quick wash up, change some of our clothes, rest some, and leave town thing. I went in and did my thing as well as Pete. We both sat and talked to the girls. Scott gets cleansed up and goes out to the van to put his little cleaning supplies way. He comes back into the ground level apartment and his faced is pale. He says, "Someone broke into our van, they stole everything... They got EVERYTHING!" We went outside and they actually left my cassette tapes I brought for the tour alone, but yup, besides that they got everything! They had broken through a little triangle window on the passenger side and reached in and opened the big van door on the side and cleaned us out. We called the cops but they acted like they could give two shits. We asked around and people told us our stuff would end up in pawn shows after a while as most people in the area we were in stole for drug money.

Since it happened to a few other touring bands that we knew of something told me you had some thieves keeping an eye on a club when an out of state band pulls in. After the show if the band stays in town you clean them out.

On the way up home we all could do nothing but laugh at how much room we had in the van without all our shit in it. But there were times that the laughter wasn't enough to keep me wondering how hard was it going to be to do this full time? This was not a great way to continue our touring full time. Years later when hurricane Katrina hit the area, I wondered if somewhere boxes of Oblivion shirts and CD's were floating in the ocean.

The worse of it was feeling like nothing we had could be secure as well as Scott had just made his own guitar and that was taken. We still went to the next show in Indiana, which was the Sloppypoolza festival, which had plenty of gear around. We all came back into town and several bands including a greatly underappreciated Chicago band Lynards Innards threw a benefit for us, which helped some with us being able to buy new instruments. From that point on we usually had one person sleep in the van, which was usually Scott.

The next time we played The Big Easy which was one of the few times we ever played with a known band in The Bouncing Souls, we said our goodbyes and got the hell out of dodge before anyone could take our life away again.

That fall the KISSS thing was helping as an outlet for stupid fun, as now Oblivion as fun as it still was, was also a job and business in some ways.

1996 closed out with us and our new gear playing various weekend shows away. Back home I had now proposed to my girlfriend (with no plans of marriage any time soon) and moved into an apartment with her. On New Year's Eve, I would go see Cheap Trick and curse them for igniting this rock and roll fire in me some 15 years before. A fire that kept burning me over and over, but I still had hope my light would somewhat shine soon enough.

1997 started with me trying to work as much as possible as a day care helper, bartender and DJ, what a mix! With only playing some weekend shows I had gathered my strength back and was looking forward to going back onto the road. Brian would send us east again in March for a two and a half week tour. We liked the east coast so much better than the west. We had many friends in New Jersey and it was becoming a second home for the band. We also found that the smart-ass attitude that the east coasters have fit better with our Chicago personalities than the laid back California thing. And the biggest reason was that the drives between the cities were much, much shorter than out west. We could save money on gas and were able to not only have our taco bell meal but often after the shows go and make spaghetti at which ever house we crashed at. The east coast seemed easier to get shows on as well. It sucked having days off. Days off meant you only spent money and didn't have a chance to earn any. We once had one day off in Indiana in which the person's house we were crashing at was gone all day so the night before we rented six dumb movies to keep us all busy. We all played a game where we had to watch all six in a row, no breaks, only getting up to use the bathroom. It was the worse movie experience I ever had in my life. A person never needs to see six movies in a row. Not even if you were going to do a Star Wars day. We also had two days off in Georgia where we all sat in this poor guy's living room and took over his TV. I remember his roommate going to work and then coming back at night telling us we all were in the same exact same spots on the couch as when he had left. He was most likely correct.

But other times you were spoiled, as the bass player for Humble Beginnings was a jersey kid whose mom was well off and had us crash at her place to use a home base for a series of shows. We were doing a split 7-inch with his band as well. We went off in his car one night to cruise the upscale town when a cop pulled us over. He informed the cop (who couldn't care less) that it was Oblivion in his car and we were on tour, as if that meant anything to the officer. He let us go probably thinking we were all special in another way. Gabe now fronts the hit dance pop band Cobra Starship (Snakes on a Plane) and hopefully is staying away from those Jersey cops.

Oblivion wouldn't go back out on the road until July which gave us two months to go into the studio and complete some of the compilation 7- inch records we had going on with Humble Beginnings, one with Apocalypse Hoboken, and what would be our last Johann's Face release, a split with another local band, God's Reflex that featured the two song combo of "The Day the Calvary Got Gum Cancer" and "The Rock Game," which Pete wrote about his feelings of the industry and what we were experiencing. It was our last for Johann's as we soon started to feel like we were not a priority for the label. Mark and Gar had a lot of bands and we didn't want to wait to put out another release. We also had some shows were people didn't get our CD's or they were out of stock. We wondered how hard they were working for us as we felt like we were doing our best for the label with being the only band constantly on the road and promoting it all. We started talking about simply rereleasing our first two records ourselves onto one disc. We also started talking about maybe finding another label to work with. The first that came to my mind was Dr. Strange who had shown some interest in the band back when I was in The Bollweevils.

I had not wanted people to think the only reason Oblivion got onto a label was through me. I already felt bad that at some shows on the road the listing for the bands would say Oblivion (featuring the Bollweevil's drummer) as well as one night it simply listed The Bollweevils instead of Oblivion. Pete and Scott always took it in stride and never complained but only joked about it. But now I had felt like enough time had passed and since the weevils were no more maybe doc would be the new home. We talked about doing a slit cd with another Dr. Strange band Man Dingo to feel out the label.

We had plenty of time to talk about everything as we spent July on the road. I was glad to be back out as the road, served in my mind, as the road to success. A slow bumpy painful road, but a road to success none the less. That summer I would move from one apartment I could barely afford to another. I got a raise at the daycare - I was now a preschool teacher of sorts for a class of the worst behaved kids. Basically I was a prison guard for preschoolers, bit I could use the extra 50 cents an hour. I also stopped bartending and cut way back on my DJ'ing to give myself a well needed brake from going out all the time. With the drop of the tip money I was doing my best to not dip into my small savings of a $3,000 left from my UPS days. Oblivion was doing great in the local all age punk scene, which by now had become a safe suburban ice and clean scene. In the city we had the fireside bowl to play whenever we wanted to. We tried a few over 21 shows at places like the Empty Bottle in the city, but we never seem to go over to that crowd. It was becoming annoying as I was a 26 year old playing in front of teenagers and the over 21 crowd simply was mostly too mature for this silly rock band. One night in my frustrations of the college cool kids scene I took up the stage persona of Bono (who I felt like they all still worshipped) and in between songs would come around from behind my drum set and do Bono like things like tell the people to let I fly as I had attached a napkin to a drum stick to recreate the famous "Sunday Bloody Sunday" video scene. Again, this mostly just entertained us as the club was already pissed off because we had played a party just hours before and they had some dumb rule where the band couldn't play any local shows within a week or two of their Empty Bottle performance. For us a simple loft party didn't count as a club show, but whatever. My in between song antics were becoming just as fun for me as playing the drums at times. My on the road antics would be the same as it seemed the crowd ate it up when we made fun of them. Unless it was Ken Weevil as we were on the Doctor Strange tour and as mentioned earlier in this here book, a drunk Kenny (who was on the tour with his band The Feds) didn't take too kindly to us playing an intro to a Bollweevil song. We got the last laugh as we kicked ass on our last show of the tour in Florida bands shouldn't be in a competition with one another, but sometimes it just happens. We were a tight touring band and a tight band of brothers who too our matters to the stage. Our stage.

The year would go into the home stretch being home more than anyway getting a little frustrated at our situation, but at least being home meant that we could earn some money at our odd jobs. I was hoping no one was getting too attached to money, as I really wanted to go back out on the road. It sucked leaving my fiancée, but I wanted to get this hard part over with so soon, hopefully soon it would all pay off in better record sales and better shows on the road. The scene its self was still growing, Green Day oddly enough with heir slow song classic, "Good riddance-time of your life..."was keeping the punk scene still in the mainstreams eyes. Even once dead bands like the Misfits were getting back together granted with a new singer to try to cash in on all this punk attention. Not all punks were doing great though as some that went to major labels were now being forgotten like Jawbox, Jawbreaker, Samiam, and Johann's Face Record's old Smoking Popes. Some of the revolution was over. The mainstream audience was going back to boy bands, and the punk crowd was shrinking and growing up to a degree. Closer to home we heard the devastating news of our label mates and at times touring partners Cletus having had their guitar player Kevin commit suicide. I felt for the guys in the band as they all were great and the family part of being on the label seemed to slowly fade away after that.

On Halloween we played a show with Apocalypse Hoboken. I remember having to change for it at the day care and running out to my car before any of their parents could see that they were trusting the care of their children to a guy wearing ripped up fish nets and black panties. We were going as the oblivion from the record cover of our split. It would be one of the most rowdy shows we ever played. The packed crowd in the suburbs was eating up both bands with. The kid who rented the hall even went out and got these huge security dudes. During our set I went up to one of these giants and told him in a band rock star English accent that I didn't want any of the peasants (crowd) near my drums. Soon after I saw this big black body builder type forcing the skinny white kid off the stage area, I had to run over and tell his I was only messing around before the kid was broken in half. Whenever a show had any form of security I did my best to watch out for the crowd. I was glad my joke didn't go too far.

Pete and I at one show at the Arlington Heights VFW decided to be our own security and in between songs we picked out the youngest smallest shyest girl and would force her out of the hall saying she was causing too much trouble. The joke got old on the crowd but never on us as we continued to do it after every song. I loved that hall as it to entertain myself I could ricochet my drum sticks off the corner of the wall and then back into my hands for a cool trick. Again, when you aren't getting laid or rich for being a rocker, you gotta' come up with something to entertain yourself behind those drums.

Speaking of sex, since my relationship for the most part was awesome I was finding it hard to draw any inspiration from our songs of being social losers. With being away from each other a lot, when we were near things were pretty darn good. I wouldn't have to look far though for inspiration to hit the drums hard as my frustrations about making music a career was always there. It was starting to feel like here we are this now "older" band. We can't seem to break into the larger crowds and can't get a big brake on the road, what is our future. I entered 1998 not really knowing how much longer we could all hold on.

With being an older band now we decided we needed to do what all older bands seemed to do. We would put together a compilation of all our early singles and unreleased tracks. I also got a call from a show promoter Dave who asked if I would be willing to open for hardcore punk legend Kevin Seconds who was coming to the Fireside Bowl on an acoustic tour.

I said "Yes," as I would do anything for money and then told my fiancée the news. When she asked what the heck would I do, it was when the thought first hit me, "yeah what the fuck will I do".

I quickly called back the promoter and asked what he wanted me to do?

He thought that since I was never at a lost for stupid things to say when I came around my drums to talk to the crowd in Pete or Scott's mic, that maybe I could do a spoken word. Umm.

"Wow," I thought to myself, "Spoken word, that is for intellectuals and people like Henry Rollins and the sort. People who have something to say. My little talking in between songs was just a chance to get up off the drum stool, stretch and say something stupid to poke fun of it all as Pete and Scott tuned between songs. My first reaction was no, but then I thought what the fuck. Sometimes in life ya' gotta go for it. I wasn't sure what "it" was but I agreed to do the performance. I was getting bored with the Fireside shows so maybe this would kick start something in me anyway. For the next few weeks I would write down anything I thought would be funny to say, as I wanted for the kids to get out of school. I had seen a few spoken word performances and they always went political and how we should over throw the government or refuse to take showers, something punk like that. I wanted to be different, a kind of like punk rockers playing acoustic guitar different, except different.

I came up with about 30 minutes of stupid thoughts, stories and on the night of the show got as drunk as I could at the bar. I remember that the normal sound person wasn't there, and this riot girl type was. "Shit" I thought she is going to kill me after the first few sexist jokes.

I better ease into this and make fun of my speech stutter first away to clear the air. Already my piece of paper with all my big time jokes was turning out to be useless. I walked over and made small talk to the sound girl and reminded her I was just a dumb drummer, and for her not to take anything personal. She actually ended up laughed more than most of the crowd that night. I talked about the Atari 2600, food, playing drums, and embellished a few road stories and made it through my first comedic set. I was told some guys from a pc hard-core band left after my first few jokes about sex, so I knew I did my job. As I walked out, Kevin Seconds remarked how much he liked it and that it was a nice change of pace from the normal spoken word artist that opened for his acoustic act. That, along with the laughter of most of the 100 or so people in attendance, made me feel jolly good. It also set a thought in my mind that maybe I could do spoken word/stand up, a thought that would never really come out again until 2006 when I agreed to do a short stand-up act for a work party/talent show night. In a non-related event I lost that job months after my routine of making fun of my managers.

I would release a cassette of that night called *Occupation Jackass*, which was a take- off from the late great George Carlin record called *Occupation Fool*. I would sell some at shows here and there but mostly gave away most of the 400 or so I had made. In the months after that night people would yell out "Jackass!" at the oblivion shows and in some strange way I felt loved.

The band Cletus was back with a new guitar player and as much as it was awesome to play with them again, the Johann's family was splitting as the core of bands who all were releasing music back in 1995 were now mostly looking around for other labels.

Oblivion had no plans to go back out for a tour at all until summer. It was killing me. I quickly got back with Brian the booker and we expanded our DJ'ing a little from Club Foot to now one-nighters at other places like Delilah's and the Metro. It wasn't enough to keep me happy, as I really wanted to get back onto the road with the band. Pete had a good job now doing freelance computer work and Scott had joined a crew of movers for Graebel Van Lines. It was a crew of guys from bands and other misfits. Mark and Gar from Johann's Face helped out along with Steven the bass player in No Empathy. Scott asked me to join as I would be making more money and told me that the owner of the crew was totally cool about letting guys go to tour whenever they wanted to. When I was on an unpaid two day leave at the day care for leaving a kid on the bus in the parking lot (never saw the little shit hiding in the back seats), I simply left and started working as a mover. It took a while to get used to real manual labor again as being a mover can really kick you in the ass day after day after day.

People would ask us all the time when we showed up, "ok, you guys are the movers, I thought you would be bigger?" as we took over their house and packed up or unloaded all their belongings.

The cool thing was that the head guy Pat, was cool with us asking off whenever we wanted to. So I had a job, a band in full swing, and was getting enough to cover rent and some months actually buy a few records. Life was going good.

Then my hand almost fell off.

I was at a moving gig at a library in Evanston when this idiot from another moving crew was pushing this metal shelving way too fast and I was trying to keep it from falling off the walking board of the truck when my hand got smashed between a sharp metal shelve already on the truck. I felt cool air and though, fuck all my fingers just came off. But then I looked at my bloody hand I could see all my fingers and saw my ligaments my hand was still there, it was just opened up. I took my other hand and closed it and was soon then rushed to the nearby hospital by the guy whose only request is that I don't bleed in his car.

I am not sure what people must have thought seeing this bloody hand being held out the window waving in the wind as this piece of shit tiny car raced down the highbrow streets of Evanston, Illinois

I spent the next 11 weeks rehabbing my hand. At that time Oblivion carried on our previously booked shows with Craig the guitarist/singer of the local punk band Mushuganas playing drums. I showed up to one and played the tambourine with one hand. Kind of like a punk rock Davey Jones except different.

Those 11 weeks were the only time I could remember not having a job to go to. I made this make shift holder for my play station controller so I could still play video games with my good left hand to kill the time. There was only so much Oprah a man could watch ya know. So in the end it wasted a summer and I lost 8% or so of movement in my fingers on my right hand. The damage could keep the 10% or so hearing loss I would later discover I had company. Hearing loss sucks, as it means you will spend the rest of your life saying the word "What" a hell of a lot. The hand injury also made me start to think to myself, what if this rock and roll thing doesn't happen, or that I couldn't do it? Well, I had already lived longer than I thought I would anyway.

When my hand finally healed oblivion hit the studio for a few days to start to record a full length that we would put out one way or another. We also had our first two records out on our *Super Saver Series CD* which we put out on our own record label PBS records. The compilation disc of all our singles and unreleased stuff *Suckers from the Start* come out on local Sinister Records and that was doing a good job of keeping our name out there and holding people off until we could come up with something new. I still think we should have gone with our original plan of calling it *Songs from Stan's Knob*.

We had this thing where we would keep naming our full lengths a name starting with then letter "S." I came up with it and really wasn't sure why the guys agreed to it. I think Pete came up with suckers, as it also could have been a takeoff on Sludgeworth's comp CD, *Losers of the Year*. Suckers has some great live tracks and as well as us doing various cover songs from Devo and AC/DC (how we started some years ago) and metal tunes like Twisted Sister's "Burn in Hell," Metallica's "Whiplash," Van Halen's "Ice Crème Man" and Iron Maiden's "The Trooper." One could never tell that we were raised on that metal shit eh? Now a days this 26 song CD is almost impossible to find, which is a crying shame.

Since I went from making eight bucks an hour to a whopping twelve, I was now able to pay for more groceries, sometimes pick up all the rent, and live a somewhat normal life, but that is not at all what I wanted. The year closed out with the members of KISSS going to see the real recently united Kiss at the All State Arena in Rosemont, IL. What a sight that was. Watching Kiss, I now knew my shinny rock star dream was dead, but couldn't I at least be a broken star rocker on the road, I had to get back on the road as this weekend warrior crap was supposed to be behind us now. There were talks of festivals like this newer Warped Tour that some bands were gaining some big audiences on. Oblivion always like the idea of a three band show in a dark smelly club, so we often passed on any festival invites, and never looked into touring with the Warped Tour or any other festivals.

1999 would start with us doing the weekend warrior thing mostly. One night while DJ'ing with Todd Pott (Apocalypse Hoboken) at Club Foot we talked about Oblivion's frustrations with trying to find a label. He suggested I get in touch with this guy Virgil from Colorado. Virgil had set up some shows for us on the road and had always liked the band but I wasn't sure how serious he was in stating a record label. After a few emails (yup, emailing was entering the scene finally) he had me sold. He was very enthusiastic and also had a way to get our cd to Japan. I had always wanted to play overseas. Oblivion had played all 48 continental states and was looking to expand besides playing up in Ontario. I really wanted to go to Europe or to Japan where many of the bands I loved like Cheap Trick had hit it big. As I brought up touring overseas to Pete he was against it as his reasoning was that if we get lost in the USA at least we could eventually find our way home. And that over in a foreign land we would be fucked if we broke down financially or emotionally. I still wanted more and often Scott and I, as we would head off to our moving jobs, would start growing frustrated in the band not touring as much. We would day dream and plan these imaginary worldwide tours filled with plenty of Euro girls and big crowds. You had to do something besides diesel gas fumes and lift heavy sleep sofas all damn day.

Our split CD on Doctor Strange came out to very little fan affair and we knew that label was too back logged to continue on so Virgil's Suburban Home Records it would be for Oblivion. Brian, our booker, had his hands full with planning shows for the red hot Fireside Bowl among other things and he also had burnt out on booking tours for us. Virgil could book a tour and put our next cd out. Things were looking up again. My dream wasn't dead yet even though I felt it slipping away, which pissed me off. I had already compromised from being a rock star to just being a guy who plays drums for a living, what more did the music gods want from me?

We played a good string of hometown shows and others in the tri state area. I was noticing Pete's girlfriend at the time going along a lot more and also becoming involved in the band's activities.

From my vantage point as one-third of the band, times were a changing. We had been a band for over a long and interesting decade and had to work very hard to get anywhere. We wanted to go touring full time, but the tours weren't enough to get people living outside the Chicago area interested in us. It seemed like you had to visit a town around three times a year, and we were doing it only once, if that. Scott and I, at the end were working as movers and our boss was cool with letting us go off whenever. But Pete had a good gig, which he still has at State Farm. And really, it is a hard choice to leave a good job for a tour that most likely will be like all the others in which we have some good shows in front of a few hundred people and some shows in front of the soda machine and the pissed off club owner who has no paying customers coming through his doors.

Our relationships were also like a worn down marriage. We all had our highs and lows and as much as we didn't want our personal relationships with our girlfriends or whomever to get in the way, they did.

It happens to many bands.

My fiancée, searching for a better life, had sort of broken up with me in the summer of 1999. If I was a wise man I would have said good grief, and went on with my life chasing the next cute girl at a show. But I felt that a four and a half year relationship was worth saving. So after a few relationship counseling sessions I found myself back with the girl who would later leave me again after a short year of marriage anyway. Go figure. Filed in my head was the fact that the band won't tour, I needed to save my relationship, and Pete's relationship was sort of bumming me out. I actually had to check in with his girlfriend a few times to see if we as a band were able to play a show. That is a bad deal. It was hard enough at that time getting all three of us in a room to talk about anything band related, other than trying to have to make us all happy, plus others. I had also, for some reason, seen Scott and Pete grow apart from the close friends they were just years before. I blamed myself for them drifting apart even though I wasn't sure how I did it.

When I joined the band in 1988 these two were different but had a solid friendship. As they both went to separate college, I think they both became a little more different, and throughout the years the band and music seemed to be the only thing they had in common. I went from being closer to Scott to closer to Pete to at the end feeling closer to Scott. So all in all it seemed things were different and I always respected bands that went out on top. I used to point at bands like Jane's Addiction, but they have come back a million times over.

I was a nervous wreck during that summer. One night my fiancée ran into the bathroom after I passed out and collapsed due to a panic attack and exhaustion. All I remember was looking at the shower head and then all of a sudden the cold feeling of the bottom of the bathtub all around me. A few days later another attack came when I was trying to go down an escalator to board the blue line on the el train. I couldn't see the steps below me and was holding up a very pissed off sea of people behind me. I was an emotional mess about my dream possibly coming to an end. I was meant to do this for a living, what was happening?

As I waited in my car one day in the suburbs for the moving truck to come, I thought long and hard about it all. I sat in this large parking lot alone. I thought to myself, was it finally over? Could there be life after Oblivion? Where my dreams all gone? I had these dreams since childhood and now where they finally fading away? Fuck. So many thoughts racing around in my head, and I knew they all lead to me needing a major change in my life to stay sane.

I remember driving in the van coming home from some college show a week later telling Pete and Scott that I was very interested in moving away and starting a new life. I told them that I recently visited Florida, and that maybe I would move there to see if I could help out at this cat sanctuary I visited on my trip. I had always liked animals more than most people anyway. I thought also moving to Florida would add something in to my soon to be dead relationship. And also because I thought Pete wasn't having fun with Scott or me anymore. No one wants the band to feel like a letdown. I didn't tell them I was quitting or anything about the band, other than I was moving away. I knew what it meant, as we always knew the band would be us three or nothing.

I had also seen other newer bands like almost instantly get huge crowds and have doors opened for them. We had been working our asses off for 10 years plus and didn't seem to have that spark that some others had. We were too strange to appeal to the masses right away. We had to grow on people, and you did that by touring. Touring was something that seemed to be behind us now. As I mentioned my feelings, neither had anything to say really, almost like they both knew the band was on limited time anyway. After that we did a short tour for Suburban Home Records in the Midwest and West Coast. We then came home to do a few shows and then our goodbye show in March of 2000. The final nail in the coffin of my rock and roll dream.

Oblivion played its final show. On the way to the show my friend Glenn who had been there from the start back in the late 80's, along with John and Bohus with their cameras filmed the opening scenes for "Swan Remains the Same" which would be the VHS/DVD of our last show. Only a few copies were given to the band and film makers, but I wish I had the money to release it now. We did parody type scenes inspired by Led Zeppelin's movie *Song Remains the Same*. Like we did a decade ago, we got off on poking fun at the mega bands and music establishment that punk hated. It would be Zeppelin that would have the last laugh on me, as they of course made it while here I was sending my musical dream off to crash like a... well, like a lead zeppelin. That night was a great fun filled evening at the Fireside Bowl. A packed, energetic crowd saw us off as we played for over an hour and tried to please everyone, including ourselves for a final time. I wore a black shirt with the words "Thank You" on it. I could say nothing more. These people had provided me with one hell of a ride. I, like usual, played too fast and the long list of songs soon became shorter and shorter. We finally got to do "Day Job" close to the record version which included my moronic guitar solo. A friend Brandon from the band Sidecar, jumped in playing drums without missing a beat. I took my junky guitar and strummed the strings not knowing what I was doing, just like on the record. The crowd reached up for me and I enjoyed being the center of attention. I wondered why the hell I took up drums so many years ago, as the front of the stage is where the action was.

As the show concluded with the song "Mauryland" I fell back into the crowd as they held me over their heads for a while. Someone pulled me down and kissed me on my lips and told me it was all she could do to thank me for being in such a cool band all these years. I felt like a part of me was dying that night. Also a part of my drum set would be gone as I promised a kid there he could take my bass drum head which featured our name in the band Queen's style with the royal coat of arms. (Hey kid, if you are reading this now, I really would love that drum head back if you no longer want it.) I got home that night and stayed up all night unable to sleep. I was nervous about my wedding in a week, I was nervous about moving, I was nervous about life without Oblivion.

As I write this I am still 50/50 on my choice, but life is full of good and bad choices, you just go on. I wasn't sure that after moving to Florida if we would play like once a year or something, as I didn't want it all to be over. I knew Oblivion as I knew it, the three idiots on the road having the time of their lives was over. I knew the early years of our artsy fartsy friends and demo tapes were over. And I knew my childhood dream, the only thing I ever felt strongly about, was also over. But we could still play every once in a while knowing it wasn't really Oblivion, but just us three friends playing like we did years ago in 1988.

We would get back together in summer 2001 for a reunion show of sorts at the Cubby Bear right across from the legendary Wrigley Field. It is also a half block north from the former spot of our favorite club to play, The Wrigley Side. It was only a little over a year since the final show, but I think we agreed to do it so soon after our demise as Sludgeworth was on the bill also reuniting along with another past local favorite, The Fighters. We did not play that well, and the overall feel of the show wasn't as good as we thought it would be. I think we all secretly hoped this would not be the last time us three gathered on stage. After that, we would communicate through emails. Myself, and then soon after Scott, had to go through divorces which suck the life out of you. I was living in a trailer in Tampa, Florida inside an animal rescue for exotic big cats like lions and tigers. My only connection with the Chicago punk world I left behind were the few reviews I did for Punk Planet and maybe once a year going to see some band I knew play a Florida show on their tour. I wished I was still in the scene as I watched Chicago bands like Alkaline Trio, Rise Against, and The Methadones come through town. I was cleaning up animal poop and had replaced my music dream with trying to save all of nature. I was still the little punk as I worked for charities and non-profits and never got any type of job working for the man. Punk rock had left me always questioning authority and asking why? And that was not a bad thing at all. Punk rock left me with the drive to Do It Yourself, and make things possible. Punk rock had given me power. I felt bad for leaving the scene and for leaving something that I felt gave me so much.

Years later in December 2006, we played our second reunion show at the Abbey Pub (always interesting to have yet another reunion gig at a club you never played the first time around). This show went a lot better that the reunion show in 2001 had, and felt much more like an old Oblivion show. Apocalypse Hoboken shared the bill with us, and for me it was a lot like the good old days. I remember being back stage downstairs just waiting for the "Rocky Theme" to begin so I could take the stage. I wanted that relive that musical adrenaline rush that I was missing for years. Walking out to a cheering audience filled my ego and it was game on time. We played very well, had fun with the audience, and besides the fact that Pete's ex-girlfriend (something I didn't notice at the time) was standing just feet away from him acting as stage security that night, everyone had a great time. While walking through the crowd during Hoboken's set, I was asked a few times if Oblivion had any future? I was personally looking forward to moving back to Chicago. It was in the back of my mind...what if? When I moved back to Chicago, Pete was involved very much with his band Mexican Cheerleader and Scott was not doing much guitar stuff. I wanted to do another reunion show, but nothing felt right for Pete, and after telling him a few times that I felt like there was always more left for us to do, the time never came. We all did meet up for Scott's going away party when he moved out West in 2012. I hung out that night mostly with Pete and our friendships were still there. We laughed at all the same dumb stuff we joked about on the road years ago.

It was the last time all three of us have ever been in the same room.

"So you want to be a rock and roll star"

The Byrds.

Looking back 20 years after the fact, would I have done anything differently?

What if we stuck it out just a few more years, and the internet could have helped us out, seeing that we drew a fan base full of geeky computer kids. What if we went on a Warped Tour and played to larger audiences? What if we recorded at different places with different people for different record labels? You could drive yourself crazy with what if's, and you should never let them get in the way of the fun and reality of what actually was.

Well, if playing rock music for a living is your dream, then I would suggest more than a little luck has to be on your side. Of course from the start it doesn't hurt to make connections. Many a band has one member that has some uncle or friend of their fathers working in the biz. I can't tell you how many punk bands we came across that were from the upper class income level or had some member using their trust fund to pay for their van and tour. It is hard to make it starting from nothing at all. One of my faults was that I was hoping things would fall into place with hard work. It also helps to network. Something I didn't do with in the biz. My main concern was making the people who came to see the band have a good time. And not shaking hands before and after the show and kissing ass. What? Kissing ass in punk rock... ha ha if you only knew. The music might be a little different than the mainstream sounds, but much of the business is the same rock game.

That would make a catchy song title eh?

I am talking about back in the 90's to when some bands were trying to stay off the majors and do things their own way. I looked at it as the majors were a business, a corporation. Why did we need to have a bunch of suit and tie guys telling us what direction to take our band? Why would we want to be controlled by a business?

If you ever get a chance, check out the movie Artifact by the band 30 Seconds to Mars. It gives a nice honest view of the business these days. Nowadays, no one really cares, as much of the music business is dead. No one sells records anymore. They hope to make money by touring and selling t-shirts, or overpriced meet and greets.

Don't get me wrong, it wasn't all jaded, many of the people Oblivion and The Bollweevils worked with were decent people. There are kids that would use their college money to put out records by bands they knew wouldn't sell just in hopes that someone would get it and like the same band that they felt needed more attention.

Oblivion often in our late years fell into the category of the band that the few wished the many would like. We were a cult band so it seemed. Who knows if we gained national popularity, if those same people would have turned on us? Now when people tell me they like the band, it means a lot. I think of all the things people listen to, and if 20 years after the fact they still like some songs we did, then I guess we did something right. I guess everything including Oblivion for some, has its place.

As for drumming after Oblivion, I played in a few bands after I moved to Tampa in 2000 to help at the big cat sanctuary. I did my time in a messed up psychotic punk band called Pig Pen in which the guys wore pig noses (of which I refused). I then joined an alternative rock band called Life of Pi. (Named after the book as the movie would come out a decade later) The band could be described as Weezer meets Dinosaur Jr., and it was a nice change of pace so to speak from the fast paced punk I was used to. We made two CD's and had a song that was voted local song of the year, but due to singer ego disease we never went past local gigs and playing SXSW. I formed another band with a new guitar player and the two guys from Life of Pi, but it didn't last long. After finally moving back to Chicago in 2008, I drummed and recorded an EP for the horror punk band Venom Lords (featuring Dan from Not Rebecca) for a year. It all has been fun in its own way, but nothing will ever come close to the times I had in Oblivion and the pursuit of my musical dream.

So who am I to tell you what to do? If you want to be in a band then go for it. You just might have some of the best times of your life, like I did. You might even one day have enough experiences to fill up a book.

Thanks to everyone that played a part however small or big in my musical journey. To all the people that supported the bands I was in, your enthusiasm never went unnoticed or unappreciated!

Thanks to Chuck Uchida and all those who helped me go for my dream. Thanks to Daryl, Bob, Ken Bollweevil and everyone I met through being in that band.

Extra special big sloppy kiss thanks goes to my brothers in crime Pete and Scott Oblivion, two friends I was lucky enough to enjoy most of this wild ride with.

Thanks also to those in my life now, all the animals who keep me sane, and of course my wife Pudn' (Bridget) who puts up with me talking about the good ol' days.

8 months ago, I took a big pile of gig flyers, photos, and tour diaries, dumped them out on the floor and did my best to sort out all the memories good and bad. I hope you enjoyed the result.

-Brian

Made in the USA
Charleston, SC
03 November 2014